"*I find the enlightening quotes and anecdotes contained in* Bottled Wisdom *much like peanuts on a bar. You can't just read one of them, you devour 'em, by the handful. This book should be required reading for the rite of passage as it contains the bottled wisdom of the ages, uttered by those of many ages, for the benefit of all ages.*

I have spent the better part of my life behind bars, and reading the book Bottled Wisdom *cover to cover makes me darn proud I did. The noble Mark Pollman is the undisputed Spirit Laureate. He has ably accepted the mantle of spokesperson for every publican and barkeep who ever strapped on an apron and doled out the good stuff.*

One note of caution, do not pick this book up when you are hurried and pressed for time."

Robert Plotkin

"*Well....this most certainly should be the Spirited Quote and Anecdote Book for the next century. Pollman has done one hell of a job with his tome on Drink Dialog. Belly up to the book, people!*"

Brian F. Rea

Bottled Wisdom *is a grand and continuing draught of your favorite beverage. It's for the quaffer, the non-quaffer, the former quaffer, the never-quaffer ... an assemblage of hilarity, wit, mirth and knowledge which left me saying to myself 'I didn't know that every second page Mark Pollman has the gift of the great tellers of stories' and if you don't buy this engaging book, your funny bone will get osteoporosis.*"

Malachy McCourt

This collection ... is a treasure of wit and pith and...a celebration of life and good times, a marvelous collection... ."

Richard Whittingham

"*If y[...] [...]ift a glass or [...]lman, the ne[...] [...]ading this delign[...] [...] [...]f quotes he's gathered on the topic of [...].*"

James Charlton

WILDSTONE MEDIA

Bottled Wisdom

COMPILED AND EDITED BY MARK POLLMAN

WISDOM

OVER 1,000 SPIRITED QUOTATIONS & ANECDOTES

Illustrations by Todd J. Reigle

"Tina"

Thanks for being part of

Mark Poll

09/23/06

My Food & Beverage Family!

 # See pg 130

& Go USA!

394.1   Pollman, Mark, 1945
POL.   Bottled Wisdom : over 1,000 spirited quotations & anecdotes /
         Mark Pollman. - St. Louis, Mo. : Wildstone Media, ©1998

           160 p.: ill.
           Includes index

           Summary: A compilation of over 1,000 quotes, toasts, anecdotes
         and sayings on the drinking experience.

           ISBN 1-882467-25-6

           1. Drinking of alcoholic beverages - Quotations, maxims, etc.
         2. Liquors - Quotations, maxims, etc.   I. Title

         HV5001   394.1'3_dc20

For information on this title
or any of our other titles,
call Wildstone Media
1-800-296-1918
or write us at
P.O.Box 511580   Saint Louis, MO 63151

Printed in U.S.A.

WILDSTONE MEDIA

INTRODUCTION

Somewhere within the great society of drinkers is a group of us that finds a kind of ecstasy in approaching the bar, taking a seat and awaiting recognition from the person who will uncork the genie.

The bar is a magical place presided over (in the best of circumstances) by a high wizard, someone who knows why he is there and knows what we pursue. He channels power and weaves it, if he knows how, into and around us. He, and I speak of the women as well, is one of life's most important people. Most bartenders enjoy the work, but many consider it something to do until they get a "real job." And yet, like the warm light of home shining through a snowy night, the truly great bartender comes along, walks among us, gives and takes and shares and multiplies the gifts with which he or she has been blessed. Mark Pollman is one of these.

A man of strong voice and commanding presence, Mark Pollman is possessed of a dagger-sharp wit, a frightening memory and a deep and abiding love of human beings in all their glory and pain. He holds court at the Fox & Hounds, a small tavern in the Cheshire Lodge in St. Louis. Though it is a hotel bar, most of the customers are regulars, even the travelers. As he should, the bartender sets the tone, delivers the prologue, and encourages the players to perform their parts well. Taking a stool at his bar means that you are clay in his hands, but that is an experience worth having and worth repeating.

Among the many pursuits of his rich life, Mark Pollman has been collecting anecdotes, poetry, prose, and observations about drinking, drinkers and drink for years. His staggering collection of literature on the subject is dwarfed only by his collection of the world's greatest sayings on the subject, which number more than 18,000. Those of us who know Mark Pollman have waited a long time for this book. In these pages are the best of the best, distilled (if you will) for your enjoyment, and to help you sound, when you are giving that all important toast, like the erudite son of a gun that you are. These are the words of the masters, brought to you with the care and dedication of a loyal scribe, a true wizard in his own right.

Jack Kenny

When all such of us
as have now reached
the years of maturity
first opened our eyes
upon the stage of existence,
we found **intoxicating liquor**
recognized by everybody,
  used by everybody,
    repudiated by nobody.
      It is commonly entered
      into the first draught of the infant
      and the last of the dying man.
      It is true that even then
    it was known and acknowledged
    that many were injured by it;
    but none seemed to think
    the injury rose from
    the use of a bad thing,
    but from the abuse
    of a very good thing. *Abraham Lincoln* 1842

P R O L O G U E

As, in the age of reason,
most things are raised
to the position of a science,
we see no reason why
Bacchanology
(if the term please our readers)
should not hold a respectable place,
and be entitled to
its due *mead* of praise.

Henry Porter and
G. Roberts 1863

This is a sensible, even socially advanced time for any serious statement about drinking and everything that spirits encompass. Historical fact will tell you that driving while drunk is wrong, as is drunken behavior in public. Honest society has laughed at and pitied others who could not control the use of liquor correctly. But the sublime things that alcohol can do for humanity are almost inexpressible. This book is a joyous and somewhat humorous attempt to look at what some profound people have said about it.

Mankind has been using some form of alcoholic beverage since long before recorded history. Early peoples tasted some things that gave them a different type of liquid pleasure and struggled for an expression of what exactly they were experiencing. Some just uttered "Damn, that is really good!" while a very few others said phrases so to the point that we all can wonder how they could know what we were feeling.

Historians will tell you that one of the major reasons that we stopped nomadic existence was the ongoing need for a civilized glass of wine or beer. The Bible has many statements praising spirits, but the only negative things it says about them are in the misuse of alcohol and drunkenness itself.

This book addresses the person who enjoys liquor with the blessedness and the consequences that it brings. Most of you will see quite a bit of yourselves in many of these quotations. Over the years many of us have experienced some memorable situations involving drink. The entire drinking experience is one of occasional disaster but mostly majestic and righteous occurrences happen that allow us to be humans. Drink should give our lives a richer meaning as well as a feeling of expansion and freedom. Everything from one's first drink to special occasions like weddings to just a cocktail after a tough work day are reasons why alcohol will always be a part of a sensible lifestyle.

Consider this book as a way to laugh and even learn about the magic and wonderment of this form of spiritual world. Enjoy my collection of sayings. Everything here is about the entire process of drinking. The good, the bad, the stupid and the splendiferous things that happen involving the drink experience - it's all here. It's a massive part of what we are as humans and therefore making us much more than other animals.

Mark Pollman (Bacchanologist)

ACKNOWLEDGEMENTS

I have an ineffable gratitude to many people, but the following list of friends is so very special for their encouragement and spiritual enthusiasm:

My Fox & Hounds patients. (Thanks for enduring my bad jokes and 45 rejection letters - without you all this collection would not exist). From my side of the bar all y'all just get brighter and more caring.

Bill and Joan Benson who see things that I look at and still don't see.

Steve, Barb & Dan Apted, Mike McCarty, Tony Bou Aoun & the Cheshire Inn staff (this is one of the don't-miss hotels in the northern hemisphere).

Jim Prentice (still HMFIC), Mary Ann Joyce, Rosemary Markley, Guy Michaels, Carol Riley, Barbara Blackburn, Angie Haushalter, Julia Richie, Kathy Brown, Linda Alberti, Tori Kasper.

Joe Pullaro, Joe Ramatowski, Jean-Claude Mallet (the quality of bartendering in heaven went up a couple of notches when these guys entered).

Mama Clara (my best girl), brothers Carl & John, sister Sandy, my buddies Kimby and Sharon & the best nephews in the world, Justin & Christopher (someday both of your artwork and energy will be international).

Ted & Gi Heinecken (the godparents of this project), Bob McGlaughlin, Jim Carlton, Dick Whittingham, Jack Kenny, Larry Yoder, Jan & Dan Longone, Ray & Jackie Foley, Alan Eames, Robert Plotkin, Brian Rea, Bert Sugar, Malachy McCourt, Tom Burnham, William Stage, Mary McGinley and all of the booksellers (new & used) in the world.

Al & Mimi Bussen, Dan Randant, J Michael Davison and the Wildstone Media staff (46 really is a magical number).

Todd & Bonnie Reigle (gift artistry when no one else would listen).

Indy, Elsa, Jackson and every Doberman rescue person in the universe. Abused dogs are very special as are abused children.

Mostly thanks to the folks of the liquor and beverage industry (all of the bartenders, waiters, waitresses, entertainers, barbacks, managers, owners, distillers, vintners, brewers, salespeople, etc.) - your right/livelihood truly makes the world a better place!

Mark Pollman

CONTENTS

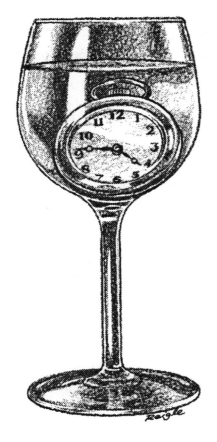

CHAPTER ONE

The Process of Drinking & Some Rules.

He that eateth well **drinketh well,**
he that drinketh well sleepeth well,
he that sleepeth well sinneth not,
and he that sinneth not goeth straight
through Purgatory to Paradise.
William Lithgow

Those who Drink

Die,

Those who do not Drink,

Die,

Why not Drink ?

Old German   Saying

Born I was to be old,

And for to die here.

After that, in the mould

Long for to lye here.

But before that day comes,

Still be BOUSING

For I know in the Tombe

There's no Carousing.
Robert Herrick

There are several reasons
 for drinking,
And one has just entered
 my head;
If a man cannot drink
 when he's **living**
How the hell can he drink
 when he's **dead?** *Anon.*

Then trust me there's
 nothing like drinking
So pleasant on this
 side the grave;
It keeps the unhappy
 from thinking,
And makes e'en the
 valiant more brave.
Charles Dibdin

I can stop drinking any time.
Important people drink.

Churchill drank.

Today is special -
a friend is in town.
Nothing is going on - why not?
Life is tragic - why not?
Tomorrow we die - why not?
John Steinbeck

If you **don't** drink;
don't smoke;
don't fool around -
you **won't** live longer -
it just seems like it!
Mark Twain

I asked my friend,
"What are your **three**
favorite pleasures in life?"
and she replied,
"A martini before and
a cigarette after."
Anon.

For gin, in cruel
Sober truth,
Supplies the fuel
For flaming youth.
Noel Coward

If the elbow had been placed
closer to the hand,
the forearm would have been
too short to bring
the glass to the mouth;
and if it had been closer
to the shoulder,
the forearm would have been
so long that
it would have carried the glass
beyond the mouth.
Benjamin Franklin

JEAN PAUL SARTRE
WALKED INTO A BAR.
"WOULD YOU LIKE A BEER?"
SAID THE BARTENDER.
"I THINK NOT."
SAID SARTRE
AND DISAPPEARED!
*Graffiti on a Philosophy
Department bathroom wall*

Said Aristotle unto Plato,
"Have another sweet potato?"
Said Plato unto Aristotle,
"Thank you, I prefer the bottle."
Owen Wister

A bumper of good liquor
Will end a contest quicker
Than justice, judge, or vicar;
So fill a cheerful glass,
And let good humor pass.

But if more deep the quarrel,
Why, sooner drain the barrel
Than be the hateful fellow
That's crabbed when he's mellow.
Richard Brinsley Sheridan

A night of good drinking
Is worth a year's thinking.

Charles Cotton

3

Let *schoolmasters*
  puzzle their brain,
With grammar, and nonsense,
  and learning;
Good liquor, I stoutly maintain,
  Gives genius better discerning.
Oliver Goldsmith

In **COLLEGE** you scorn'd
  the art of thinking,
But learned all moods
  and figures of good drinking
John Dryden

I believe more people break their brains
by drinking than study:
for tho' the latter
may be troublesome enough,
yet a book is not so hard as a bottle.
Bernard De Mandeville

Leeze me on drink, it gies us mair
Than either school or college:
It kindles wit, it waukens lear,
It pangs us fu' of knowledge,
Be't whisky gill or pennywheep
Or any stronger potion,
It never fails, in drinking deep,
To kittle up oor notion
By night or day.
Robert Burns

Drinking is in reality
an occupation which employs
a considerable portion of
the time of many people;
and to conduct it in
the most rational and
agreeable manner
is one of the great
arts of living.
James Boswell

We need to educate young people,
two-thirds of whom will drink
when they grow up,
about drinking responsibly.
  We need to teach enjoyment
of drinking for the good taste,
and the great contributions
alcohol has made to our civilization,
rather than making it a rite of passage
for adolescents who seek effect
rather than enjoyment.
  The Europeans have far fewer
problems with alcohol than we do,
because they learn to enjoy it
from childhood on.
  Our children are not allowed
to learn to deal with alcohol gradually,
they are thrust into it by their peers,
not under the supervision of adults.
No wonder they have problems coping.
Fred Eckhardt

I've always learned early in life how to handle alcohol and never had any trouble with it. The rules are simple as mud.

First, never drink if you've got any work to do. Never. If I've got a job of work to do at 10 o'clock at night I wouldn't take a drink up to that time.

Secondly, never drink alone. That's the way to become a drunkard.

And **thirdly,** even if you haven't got any work to do, never drink until it's dark.
By that time you're near enough to bed to recover quickly.

I think the danger of alcohol largely consists of this:
if a man starts to drink too early in the day,
or if he's got anything that puts a strain on him to do,
as the alcohol goes out or even while it's still in
he notices a letting down and he's tempted
to drink some more which removes that feeling
of being let down and the result is
he gets on a wheel and he drinks too much.

H. L. Mencken

The art of rational drinking is an accomplishment as indispensable as dancing or bridge, and a fair knowledge of wines and liqueurs, their provenance, characteristics, best years, etc., forms part of a gentleman's culture ... To know how to drink is as essential as to know how to swim, and one should be at home in both these closely related elements.

Each man reacts differently to alcohol; he should know before the time when, according to custom, he indulges in his first collegiate 'binge', whether liquor affects his head, his legs, or his morals; whether he sings, fights, weeps, climbs lampposts or behaves with excessive affection towards the opposite sex; whether, in short, it makes him a jovial companion or a social pest.

In vino veritas does not mean that a man will tell the truth when in drink, but he will reveal the hidden side of his character.

Frank Meier

5

REASONS FOR DRINKING

Not everybody is strong enough to endure life without an **anesthetic.**
Drink probably averts more gross crime than it causes.

George Bernard Shaw
(a teetotaler)

I wonder what pleasure men take in making beasts of themselves!

I wonder, madam, that you have not the penetration enough to see the strong inducement to this excess;
for he who makes a beast of himself gets rid of the pain of being a man.

Dr. Samuel Johnson

I drink to remove warts and pimples from the people I'm looking at.

Jackie Gleason

The *tranquilizer* of greatest value since the early history of man, and which may never become outdated, is alcohol, when administered in moderation. It possesses the distinct advantage of being especially pleasant to the taste buds.

Nathan Masor

I hate to advocate drugs, alcohol, violence, or insanity to anyone - but they've always worked for me.

Hunter S. Thompson

I only drink to make other people seem interesting.

George Jean Nathan

What it does is relax you; it frees you for a time from a *nagging* inner self and helps make the world brighter; it heightens your pleasure and makes you feel good.

Morris E. Chafetz

People drink for hereditary reasons, nutritional reasons, social reasons.

They drink because they are bored, or tired, or restless.

People drink for as many reasons as they have for wanting to 'feel better'.

Alfred Kazin

6

The mistakes made
by doctors are innumerable.
They err habitually
on the side of optimism
as to treatment,
of pessimism
as to the outcome.
'Wine? In moderation,
it can do you no harm,
it's always a tonic.
Sexual enjoyment?
After all it's a natural function.
But you mustn't over do it,
you understand.
Excess in anything is wrong'
At once,
what a temptation
to the patient
to renounce
those two life-givers,
water and chastity!
Marcel Proust

I carry on mental dialogues
with the shoots of the grapevine,
who reveal to me grand thoughts
and to whom I can retell
wondrous things.
Johann Wolfgang Von Goethe

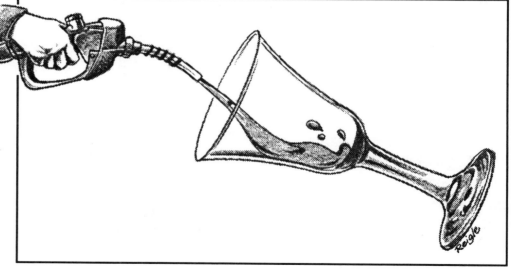

7

Liquor drinking at the end of an emotionally grueling day may have a real civilizing effect on the overtense, overwrought, over-anxious, and over-irritable husband who comes seeking rest and peace in his own home.

Here the civilizing effects (of moderate amounts) will really perform wonders in helping husbands and wives to feel tolerant and understanding of each other.

These amenities help adults generally to adjust themselves in a socially acceptable way to the stresses of our complex social situation.

Chauncy D. Leake

If liquor can overcome and suppress man's awareness of the little miseries and drudgeries in life, and thus set free and strengthen his enthusiasm for whatever dominant ideas he may cherish, and if it can lubricate the frictions and pains and bring back once again the feeling of unity and freedom of flow, then humans would be fools to ignore this aid to civilization.

Morris E. Chafetz

IT IS WELL TO REMEMBER THAT THERE ARE FIVE REASONS FOR DRINKING: THE ARRIVAL OF A FRIEND; ONE'S PRESENT OR FUTURE THIRST; THE EXCELLENCE OF THE WINE; OR ANY OTHER REASON.

Old Latin Saying

All this is so obvious that I marvel no Utopian has ever proposed to abolish all the sorrows of the world by the simple device of getting and keeping the whole human race *gently tight.* I do not say drunk, remember; I say simply tight - and apologize, as in duty bound, for not knowing how to describe the state in a more seemly phrase. The man who is in it is a man who has put all his best qualities into his shop window. He is not only immensely more **amiable** than the cold sober man; he is more decent. He reacts to all situations in an expansive, generous and humane manner. He has become more liberal, more tolerant, more kind. He is a better citizen, husband, father, friend. The enterprises that make human life on this earth **uncomfortable**, and **unsafe** are never launched by such men. They are not the makers of wars; they do not rob and oppress anyone; they invent no such plagues as income taxes, jazz and Prohibition. All the great villainies of history, from the murder of Abel onward, have been perpetrated by sober men, chiefly by TEETOTALERS. But all the charming and beautiful things, from the **Song of Songs**, to *bouillabaisse,* and from the nine *Beethoven* symphonies to the MARTINI cocktail, have been given to humanity by men who, when the hour came, turned from tap water to something with color in it, and more in it than mere oxygen and hydrogen.

H. L. Mencken

9

We hear of the conversion of
water into wine
at the marriage,
in Cana, as a miracle.
But this conversion is,
through the goodness of God,
made every day before our eyes.

Behold the rain,
which descends from Heaven
upon our vineyards,
and which enters into
the vine-roots to be changed
into wine: *a constant proof that
God loves us and
loves to see us happy.*

The *miracle* in question
was only performed to
hasten the operation,
under circumstances of necessity,
which required it.

Benjamin Franklin

The truth is that mankind,
in all ages,
especially in the cold climates,
have been at great pains
to secure for themselves
exhilarating and **intoxicating** liquors,
which cheered their spirits,
warmed their hearts and
filled their minds with joy.

Dr Henry

As long as you represent me
as praising alcohol
I shall not complain.
It is, I believe,
the greatest of human inventions,
and by far -
much greater than *Hell,*
the *radio* or the *bichloride tablet.*

H. L. Mencken

And finally, we can say that
alcohol has existed longer
than all human memory.
It has outlived generations,
nations, epochs and ages.
It is a part of us,
and that is fortunate, indeed.
For although alcohol will always
be the master of some,
for most of us it will continue
to be the servant of man.

Morris E. Chafetz

I am sure of this,
that if everybody was to drink
their bottle a day,
there would be not half
the disorders in the world
there are now.
It would be a famous good thing
for us all.

Jane Austin

10

Drink helps us
to penetrate the veil;
it gives us glimpses
of the Magi of creation
where they sit weaving their spells
and sowing their seeds of incantation
to the flowing mind.

Don Marquis

There is absolutely no scientific proof
of a trustworthy kind,
that **MODERATE CONSUMPTION** of
sound alcoholic liquor
does a healthy body any harm at all;
while on the other hand
there is the unbroken testimony
of all history that alcoholic liquors
have been used by the strongest,
wisest, handsomest,
and in every best way
races of all times.

George Saintsbury

*For a man
in his cups,
is far
more eloquent
than a man
who is not!*

*Bruce Alan
Campbell*

I can't count the number of
delectable hours I've spent in bars,
the perfect places for the
meditation and contemplation
indispensable to life ... ***The Bar*** ...
is an exercise in solitude.
Above all else, it must be quiet,
dark, very comfortable - and,
contrary to modern mores,
no music of any kind,
no matter how faint.
In sum, there should be no more than
a dozen tables, and
a clientele that doesn't like to talk.

Luis Bunuel

Human beings
are at their best
IN BARS.

Alec Waugh

11

Alcohol is nicissary f'r a man
so that now an' thin
he can have a **good opinion**
iv himself,
ondisturbrd be th' facts.
Finley Peter Dunne

A cardinal Irish rule is that
what is said when drink is taken
is never repeated the next day
or held against you.
In fact, even in court,
the best defense
the accused can offer is

"Drink was taken"

That plea will always soften
the verdict from
an Irish judge and jury.
John McCarthy

Some men
are like
musical
glasses;
to produce
their
finest tones
you must
keep them
wet.
Samuel Taylor Coleridge

Let us candidly admit that
there are shameful blemishes
on the American past, of which
the worst by far is **rum.**
Nevertheless, we have improved
man's lot and enriched his
civilization with rye, Bourbon
and the Martini cocktail. In all
history has any other nation
done so much?
Bernard DeVoto

"Ye ra-aly do think dhrink
  is a nicissry evil?"
  said Mr Hennessy.
"Well" said Mr Dooley,
"if it's an evil to a man,
  it's not nicissry,
  an if it's nicissry it's an evil."
Finley Peter Dunne

The *peculiar charm* of alcohol
lies in the sense of careless well-
being and bodily and mental
comfort which it creates.
It unburdens the individual
of his cares and fears …
Under such conditions
it is easy to laugh or weep,
to love or to hate,
not wisely but too well.
Dr Haven Emerson

Place a substantial meal
before a tired man
and he will eat with effort
and be little better for it at first.
Give him a glass of wine or
brandy, and immediately
he feels better:
you see him come to life again
before you.

Brillat-Savarin

12

In her later years,
Dr Samuel Johnson's wife
declined to sleep with her husband
because of failing health.
Some time later,
when asked what was
the greatest pleasure in life,
Dr Johnson answered,
"fucking, and the second was drinking."
He therefore wondered why
there were not more drunkards,
"for all could drink
tho' all could not fuck."   *Anon.*

After a few ounces,
the old tunes wake up,
the grandeur of the jingling anguish,
the lick and simmer of language,
the heartbreak at the core of things …
At a certain glow-level
my brilliancies assured me
I was an angel writing in Paradise.
                                    Donald Newlove

A writer who drinks carefully
is probably a better writer.
The main effect of the grain
on the creative personality
is that it provides
the necessary sense of
newness and freshness,
without which creative
writing does not occur.
                        Stephen King

P. G. Wodehouse

Drinking makes you loquacious,
as we all know, and if what you've
got for company is a piece of paper,
then you're going to talk to it.
Just try to enunciate,
and try to make sense.
                    Madison Smartt Bell

The act of drinking

is an act which only races of ancient
lineage possess. When one makes use
of wine moderately, as with all precious
things, it is health and medicine.
It increases muscular power,
it exalts the sex drive,
it stimulates the nervous
and psychical systems.
It renders eloquence easy,
it leads to benevolence,
to good fellowship,
to forgiveness and to heroism.
                    Jack D. L. Holmes

13

If wine disappeared
from human production,
I believe there would be,
in the health and intellect
of the planet, a void,
a deficiency far more terrible
than all the excesses and deviations
for which wine is made responsible.
Is it not reasonable to suggest that
people who never drink wine,
whether naïve or doctrinaire,
are fools or hypocrites ...?
A man who
drinks only water
has a secret to hide
from his fellowmen. *Baudelaire*

There are none of us who can live
comfortably upon what we call
the necessaries of life only,
but all stand frequently in need
of other recruits.
Other creatures can labor and toil
and still continue their cheerfulness
without anything but what is just
necessary to support their binges
and keep them alive.
   This is not the case with men:
they cannot hold out without some
spirituous refreshment,
some liquor to cheer them,
that is stronger than simple water.

I cannot think that Noah was the
inventor of wine, but imagine
he was taught to make it
by the antediluvians
who were eating and drinking
and enjoying themselves
when the flood came.
The same need of refreshment
which caused the invention of wine
in that part of the world
where man was first placed
did very soon after
in other countries produce
other liquors which might
have the same effect.
W. T. Marchant

God made yeast,
as well as dough,
and loves fermentation
just as dearly as he loves vegetation.
Ralph Waldo Emerson

Eat, drink and be merry, for tomorrow ye diet.
Lewis C. Henry

14

People have discovered
many ways of gathering money
and amassing wealth,
little thinking that their
life will end and that
they will soon be laid in the grave.
Whether you're a landlord,
a duke or a king,
not a penny will accompany you
under the sod, and so, therefore,
there's no better employment
than the enjoying of life
with plenty to drink.

Riocard Bairéad

A drop now and then
is no harm when
you're in low spirits,
or have a cold.

Eugene O'Neill

"Now," says an enthusiastic American,
"I ax you fellers who is the best citizen?
him as supports Guvernment,
or him who doesn't?
Why him as does, of course.
We support Guvernment we fellars.
Every man who drinks beer
supports Guvernment - that is,
if he lickers at a licensed house.
Every blessed drop of licker he
swallows there is taxed to pay
the salary of some of them
'ere great bigwigs.
Suppose we quit drinking,
why Guvernment must fail -
it couldn't help it, nohow.
That's the very reason I drinks.
If I followed my inclernation,
I'd rather drink buttermilk
or gingerpop, or soda water.
But I lickers for the good of
my country, to set an example
of patriotism and self-denial
to the rising generation."

Anon.

George Jean Nathan
once speculated that
if O'Neill 'hadn't drunk
the way he did and mixed
with many kinds of people
in those early days,
we probably shouldn't
have had his plays.'

Donald W. Goodwin

One of the
saddest things
is that the only
thing a man
can do for
eight hours,
is work.
You can't eat
eight hours a day,
nor drink for
eight hours a day,
nor make love for
eight hours.

William Faulkner

15

When the office clock is showing
That the time is half past four,
    I feel I must be going
Where I've often gone before,
For I need no rough awakening,
    And I want no whistle's hoot,
To say my thirst needs slaking
    On the Cocktail Route.

Roland Whittle

[*The cocktail hour*]
makes the lifeward turn.
The heart wakens from coma
and its dyspnea ends.
Its strengthening pulse is
to cross over into the campground,
to believe that the world has not
been altogether lost or, if lost,
not altogether in vain.

Bernard DeVoto

When things get too unpleasant,
I burn the day's newspaper,
pull down the curtains,
get out the jugs,
and put in a civilized evening.

H. L. Mencken

A man is a fool if he drinks
before he reaches fifty,
and a fool if he doesn't
drink afterward!

Frank Lloyd Wright

When I think of the hardship
involved in only having
seven hours to drink
on a Sunday
my soul shudders.

Kevin Christopher O'Higgins

King Kelly

It depends on the
length of the game.

*(When asked if he
drank while
playing baseball)*

16

Late to bed and late to rise,
Makes you soggy and groggy
with bloodshot eyes.
Early to bed and early to rise,
Makes your girl go out
with other guys!
Bernie Candy

Max. "Say, is it too early for a drink?"
Polly. "What's early about it?
It's tomorrow in Europe
and yesterday in China."
Ruth Gordon

Will Sinclair, a prominent figure
of Fischer Island in its heyday,
was cherished for his retort
on the ridiculous query as to whether
he would care for a drink:
"The only time I ever said no to that
was when I misunderstood
the question."
Jill Spalding

WHO DRINKS?

I have
to think hard
to name
an interesting man
who
does not
drink.

Richard Burton

*I have known people
who drank secretly
and were besotted publicly.*
*George Christoph
Lichtenberg*

They drink early and late;
they consume enough beer,
wine, anise, grappa
and Fundador to put them
all into alcoholic wards,
if they were ordinary mortals;
but drinking seems to
have the effect on them
of a magic potion.

Malcolm Cowley
(on the Hemingway heroes)

Definition of diplomatic life:
Protocol, alcohol and Geritol.
Adlai E. Stevenson
(as US ambasador to the United Nations)

17

The Preservation of Man

The Horse and Mule live Thirty years,
And know nothing of Wines and Beers.
The Goat and Sheep at Twenty die
    with never a taste of Scotch or Rye.
The Cow drinks water by the ton
    and at Eighteen is mostly done.
The Dog at Sixteen cashes
    without the aid of Rum or Gin.
The Cat in Milk and Water soaks and
    then in Twelve short years it croaks.
The modest, sober, bone dry Hen
    lays eggs for nogs, then dies at Ten.
All animals are strictly dry.
    They sinless live and swiftly die,
But sinful, Ginful, Rum-soaked Men
    Survive for Threescore years and Ten
And some of us - the mighty few -
    Stay pickled 'til we're Ninety-two.

Anon.

Drinking when we are not thirsty
and making love all year round,
madam; that is all there is
to distinguish us from other animals.

Montesquieu

Too much work, and no vacation,
Deserves at least a small libation.
So hail! my friends,
    and raise your glasses;
Work's the curse
    of the drinking classes.

Oscar Wilde

The colonials (Australians)
are here at Cowes ...
their sailing performances
have been impressive,
their drinking even better.

Robert Mundle

The wine had such ill effects
on Noah's health that
it was all he could do
to live 950 years.
Just nineteen years short
of Methuselah.
Show me a total abstainer
that ever lived that long.

Will Rogers

Drinking makes
such fools of people,
and people are such fools
to begin with that
it's compounding a felony.

Robert Benchley

Pitted against hard drinking
Christians the abstemious
Mahometans go down
like grass before the scythe.

Ambrose Bierce

18

"CPO CREED"
(An Old Sailor's Creed)

A Chief Petty Officer Does Not Drink,
But Should A Chief Petty Officer Drink,
He Does Not Get Drunk,
But Should A Chief Petty Officer Get Drunk,
He Does Not Stagger,
But Should A Chief Petty Officer Stagger,
He Does Not Fall,
But Should A Chief Petty Officer Fall,
He Falls On His Left Side;
So That All Who Pass Think
   He Is A Junior Officer.

David L. Murdock
Master Chief Petty Officer, US Navy

We are fighting Germany,
Austria and drink,
and as far as I can see,
the greatest of these three
deadly foes is drink.

David Lloyd-George

When I realized that what I turned out to be was a lousy, two-bit pool hustler and drunk, I wasn't depressed at all. I was glad to have a profession.

Danny McGoorty

We like to drink, suh, and we like people who like to drink!
A Texan's admonition to an abstainer.

The South is dry and will vote dry. That is, everybody sober enough to stagger to the polls will.

Will Rogers

"My Favorite Thirst"

From the first, I had a thirst for paregoric.
Castor Oil I swallowed by the quart.
I was scarcely off the nipple,
When I searched for stronger tipple.
(I was always on the lookout for a snort.)
Oh, the dames..., they called me names.
My father whaled me, "I declare", he said,
"The lad will be a souse."
It was at my First Communion,
When with joy, I started croonin',
"Holy Moses, Dad,
The drinks are on the house."   *Anon.*

Religions change; beer and wine remain.
Hervey Allen

Woodrow Wilson:
"And what, in your opinion, is the trend
 of the modern English undergraduate?"
F. E. Smith (Earl of Birkenhead):
"Steadily towards women and drink,
 Mr. President."

19

He was a writer who drank,
not, as so many have believed,
a drunk who wrote.

James Lundquist
(On Sinclair Lewis)

Some writers take to drink,
others take to audiences.

James Thurber

A mind of the caliber
of mine cannot derive
its nutriment
from cows.

George Bernard Shaw

So take your proper share,
man of Dope and Drink:
Aren't you the Chairman
of Ego, Inc.?

W. H. Auden

No animal ever invented
anything as bad as drunkeness -
or so good as drink.

G. K. Chesterton

He was hanged that
left his drink behind him.
*(Only a man running for
his life would do so.)*

English proverb

If any of my players don't
take a drink now and then
they'll be gone.
You don't play this game
on gingersnaps.

Leo Durocher
(as Cubs manager)

It is a bad man who remembers
what went on at a drinking bout!

Greek proverb

If the husband drinks,
half the house is afire;
if the wife drinks,
the whole house.

Russian proverb

A drinking man's someone
who wants to forget
he isn't young an' believing.

Tennessee Williams

He who is master of his thirst
is master of his health.

Old French proverb

You yourself, my lord Prior,
like to drink of the best.
So does any honest man;
never does a man of worth
dislike good wine;
it is a monastical apothegm.

Rabelais

20

We're in such a slump that even the ones who are drinkin' aren't hittin'.

Casey Stengel

Bad stations and good liquor and long service
Have aged his looks beyond their forty-five;
For eight and twenty years he's been a soldier;
And nineteen months of war have made him thrive.

Siegfried Sasson

But, few countries I have observed are threatened today by one aspect of American drinking behavior which I find especially impressive and worrisome: *when many Americans drink, they behave as though they are sinning.* Therefore, drinking together is like sinning together, and this results in much guilt. …it's about time Americans stopped wasting so much of their lives worrying about sin.

Morris E. Chafetz

A waltz and a glass of wine invite an encore.

Johann Strauss

Faulkner was a big drinker, went on wild binges but he never wrote much while drunk. He and others drank to broaden their vision, their exaltation or despair, or to flee from the agony of the pure pain of creation.

William Styron

21

It was an era when parents
promised their sons gold watches
if they abstained till they were 21.
Andrew Turnbull

I love drinking now and then.
It defecates the standing pool of thought.
A man perpetually in the paroxysm and
fears of inebriety is like a half-drowned
stupid wretch condemned to labor
unceasingly in water;
but a now-and-then tribute to Bacchus
is like the cold bath, bracing and
invigorating.
Robert Burns

Men do not knowingly drink for the
effect alcohol produces on the body.
What they drink for is the brain-effect;
and if it must come through the body,
so much the worse for the body.

Jack London

At one time his drinking got all
mixed up with his health fads, and
he got it into his head that he
needed hot Scotch or champagne
or ale or beer - the formula varied
from time to time- to put him
to sleep. In a letter written for
publication in 1883, he disclaimed
being an expert on the effects of
alcohol on thinking and writing,
but he found two glasses of
champagne "the happiest
inspiration for an after-dinner
speech," he felt wine 'a clog to the
pen, not an inspiration.' and could
not write after drinking even one glass.

A Mark Twain biographer

While there were some
musicians who did a fair
amount of boozing and
whoring around and
marijuana smoking, there
was also a hell of a lot of
damn good honest jazz
being played around.
Artie Shaw

Do you remember
any great poet
that ever illustrated
the higher fields of humanity
that did not dignify
the use of wine
from Homer on down?

James A. McDougall

"LOVE, WOMEN & ALCOHOL"

Wine comes in at the mouth
And love comes in at the eye;
That's all we shall know for truth
Before we grow old and die.
I lift the glass to my mouth,
I look at, and I sigh.

William Butler Yeats

There is wan thing an' on'y wan thing to be said in favor iv drink an' that is that it has caused manny a lady to be loved that otherwise might've died single.

Finley Peter Dunne

I presunted myself at Betty's bedside late at nite, with considerbull licker koncealed about my persun.

Artemus Ward

Many a Miss would not be a Missus,
If Liquor did not add spark to her kisses.

Bill Tennenbaum

Try substituting the word 'women' for the word 'drinking' in the AA questionnaire.
Are women affecting your peace of mind?
Are women making your home life unhappy?
Do you show a marked moodiness since women?
Are women disturbing the harmony of your life?
Have women changed your personality?
Do you crave a woman at a definite time daily?
Do you require a woman next morning?
Do you prefer a woman alone?
Have women made you irritable?
Yes, yes, yes, and again yes.

Jeffrey Bernard

What, when drunk, one sees in other women,
one sees in Garbo sober.

Kenneth Tynan

The glances over cocktails
That seemed to be so sweet
Don't seem quite so amorous
Over the Shredded Wheat.

Anon.

Alcohol is like love;
the first kiss is magic,
the second is intimate,
the third is routine.
After that you just take
the girl's clothes off.

Raymond Chandler

Drinking with women
is as unnatural as
scolding with 'em.

William Wycherly

23

Alcohol was a threat to women, for it released men from the moral control they had learned from a diet of preaching and scolding from ministers and mothers alike.

Alice Rossi

A drunken woman is lost to shame.

Irish saying

She pledged him once,
   and she pledged him twice,
And she drank as a lady
   ought not to drink.

R. H. Barham

Too much drinking makes one very improper for the acts of Venus.

Aristotle

I am a stylist, and the most beautiful sentence I have ever heard is, "Have one on the house."

Addison Mizner

When asked what wine he liked to drink, he (Diogenes) replied, "That which belongs to another".

Diogenes

The rapturous, wild and ineffable pleasure of drinking at somebody else's expense.

H. S. Leigh

FREE BEER TOMORROW

McGuire Martin
McGuire's Irish Pub

Even though a number of people have tried, no one has yet found a way to drink for a living.

Jean Kerr

humanity i love you because when you're hard up you pawn your intelligence to buy a drink.

e. e. cummings

He died of cirrhosis of the liver, it costs money to die of cirrhosis of the liver.

P. G. Wodehouse

One dollar back home buys five beers. People will look at me like a rich man.

Andres Galarraga
(Montreal Expos first baseman, on his hometown of Caracas, Venezuela)

Uniting the business of the wine merchant and banker, you could manage a capital business: since for those who took yours *draughts* overnight you could reciprocate by honoring their *drafts,* in the morning.

Richard Brinsley Sheridan

There aren't many left like him nowadays, what with education and whisky the price it is.

Evelyn Waugh

24

When neebors angry at a plea,
An' just as wud as wud can be,
How easy can the barley-bree
Cement the quarrel.
It's aye the cheapest lawyer's fee
To taste the barrel.
Robert Burns

It is sweet to drink but bitter to pay for.
Irish proverb

If a person twenty years old drinks one pint of beer a day until he is sixty - bang goes £720! Why support a public-house when you might buy your own?
Advertisement in the *Dudley Herald*

If a body could just find oot th exac' proper proportion and quantity that ought to be drunk every day, and keep to that, I verily trow that he might leeve for ever, without dying at a', and that doctors and kirkyards would go oot o' fashion.

James Hogg

We must teach our children that it is not the year, the producer, or even the label that determines the quality of the wine; it is the wine in the glass, whatever the label or producer or year. It is a sin to allow a son (or daughter) to grow up thinking that because the label says

Chateau Lafite-Rothschild 1963

and costs $30 that is a fine wine. In this particular case, it is a poor wine. Drink wine, not labels.
Dr Maynard Amerine
Professor Emeritus of Enology
University of California at Davis

The man who is master of himself drinks gravely and wisely.
Confucius

Perfect knowledge and appreciation begat natural temperance.
Neil Gunn   (on abuse of his native whisky)

J.P. Morgan was once present with a group of men at a bar in the financial district. Beckoning to the waiter, he ordered a beer; at the same time, saying: "When Morgan drinks, everybody drinks." Everybody had a beer and when Morgan had finished, he slapped a dime upon the table, saying, "When Morgan pays, everybody pays."

25

Not all drinking is everyday drinking.

In everyone's life there are special occasions that call for a celebration of one kind or another.

We drink to celebrate a marriage, an anniversary or a birthday. We drink to celebrate the arrival of a child, and to celebrate a promotion to a new position. And sometimes we drink even in sorrow, when someone we love has died. On New Year's Eve we drink a toast to the year that is being born - but we think of the year that is dying, too. In fact, there is hardly any milestone in life that doesn't slip past more gracefully and memorably if we raise a glass to it.

....To drink is fine; to overdrink is pointless.

Toots Shor

Drink the first. Sip the second slowly. Skip the third.

Knute Rockne

Drink all you want,
but don't be a drunken shit.
I drink and get drunk every day,
but I never bother anyone.

Ernest Hemingway

Were I to prescribe
a rule for drinking,
It should be formed upon a saying
quoted by Sir William Temple:
the first glass for myself,
the second for my friends,
the third for good humor,
and the fourth for mine enemies.

Joseph Addison

It's a lot easier
when you're starting,
because when you're starting
you can pick your days to drink.

Bill Lee
(on the advantages of starting over relieving)

The juice of the grape is given to him that will use it wisely, as that which cheers the heart of man after toil, refreshes him in sickness and comforts him in sorrow. He who so enjoyeth it may thank God for his wine-cup as for his daily bread; and he who abuseth the gift of heaven is not a greater fool in his intoxication than thou in thine abstinence.

Sir Walter Scott

I think I am the only one of His Majesty's Ministers who has drunk a Soviet minister under a table.

Harold Wilson

Yet this is not a subject on which it pays to be either ignorant or intolerant. To know at least a little about what to drink, and when, and how, is to be a little better equipped for present-day living. Not to know, or care, is to deprive oneself of a great deal of pleasure, like not knowing or caring about anything but chopped steak and potatoes at every meal. *Sherman Billingsley*

Sometimes he varied his drinks. He liked to change. Whiskey, gin, campari, Tom Collins, tequila. He also drank different wines: Tavel, his favorite French rosé, then Chianti in the straw bottle, four or five litres with dinner. He liked to serve the wine himself. He held the bottle by the neck while he poured. This was awkward but he justified it by saying: "The bottle by the neck. Women by the waist."
Norberto Fuentes
(on Ernest Hemingway)

One of the fellows I can't understand is the man with violent likes and dislikes in his drams - the man who dotes on highballs but can't abide malt liquor, or who holds that Scotch whiskey benefits his kidneys whereas rye whiskey corrodes his liver. As for me, I am prepared to admit some merit in every alcoholic beverage ever devised by the incomparable brain of man and drink them all when occasions are suitable - wine with meat, the hard liquors when my so-called soul languishes, beer to let me down gently of an evening. In other words, I am omnibibulous, or more simply,

ombiblous.

H. L. Mencken

In drinking etiquette it is taboo not to accept a proffered drink or, for that matter, not to reciprocate. Communal drinking is characterized by a remarkable ambivalence. On the other hand, it creates fraternity among drinkers, on the other this relationship is marked by mutual caution, obligation, and competitiveness, which make it seem far less friendly. In an instant the bond can be broken and turned into its opposite, should the basic rule be violated. Anyone who refuses a drink offered him in a workers' bar may well find himself in the middle of a brawl; if he does not in turn offer a round, he makes a fool of himself.

Wolfgang Schivelbusch

27

It all depends on what you are doing with the evening. If you are watching television a friendly glass or two of beer goes well. If you are out of town it is time for a high-ball. The important thing is that these are your hours of leisure This means the drink wants to be mild, not strong, and wants to be sipped, not gulped. Things are more sociable that way.

Bob Cobb

Drink is in itself a good creature of God, and to be received with thankfulness, but the abuse of drink is from Satan, the wine is from God, but the Drunkard is from the Devil.

Increase Mather

The less I behave like Whistler's mother the night before, the more I look like her the morning after.

Tallulah Bankhead

I always keep a supply of stimulant handy in case I see a snake, which I also keep handy.

W. C. Fields

When I was two years of age she asked me not to drink, and then I made a resolution of total abstinence. That I have adhered to it and enjoyed the beneficent effect of it through all time, I owe to my grandmother. I have never drunk a drop from that day to this of any kind of water.

Mark Twain

I decided to stop **drinking with creeps**. I decided to drink only with friends. I've lost 30 pounds.

Ernest Hemingway

A heavy drinker is someone who drinks more than his doctor does.

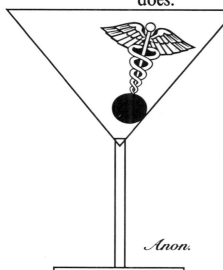

Anon.

A government advertisement in the Paris Métro when Mendes-France was trying to wean the French from alcohol to milk: *"L'alcool tue lentement"* (Alcohol kills slowly.) A wag wrote beneath it: *"Tant mieux. Nous ne sommes pas pressés."* (Fine. We're not in a hurry.)

Anon.

So what's the hurry?

Robert Benchley
(responding to a warning that drinking is 'slow poison')

One drink is plenty;
Two drinks too many,
And three not half enough.

A. Knox Haynes

They never taste who always drink;
They always talk who never think.

Matthew Prior

Not drunk is he who from the floor
can rise alone and still drink more;
But drunk is he who prostrate lies,
Without the power to drink or rise.

Thomas Love Peacock

I see where New York is going to make their nightclubs close at three in the morning, and the people are kicking about it. Well, I say they ought to close 'em. Anybody that can't get drunk by three A.M. ain't trying.

Will Rogers

29

Interviewer:
"Were you drunk at four a.m.?"
Humphrey Bogart:
"Isn't everybody?"

Humphrey Bogart

When one comes to think of it, it's odd that there should be so much admiration for prowess in drinking, which after all is merely a domestic virtue.

W. Grenfell

I don't drink any more than the man next to me, and the man next to me is Dean Martin.

Joe E. Lewis

If you can get a man drunk you find out what kind of person they really are.

Gussie Busch

What a man says drunk he has thought sober.

Flemish proverb

That I call immoderation that is beside or beyond that order of good things for which God hath given us the use of drink.

Jeremy Taylor

There are more old drunkards than old physicians.

Rabelais

I never heard praise ascribed to a drunkard, but the well-bearing of his liquor, which is a better commendation for a brewer's horse.

William Cecil

Correct not your servants when they are drunk, it shows as if you were drunk yourself.

Cleobulus

"HOW *NOT* TO DRINK"

Casey (Stengel) once told us that he didn't mind you going out with your roommate. But he didn't want four or five of us going out together because that way everybody would want to buy one round and by the end of the night we'd all be **gassed.**

Ed Kranepool
(New York Mets first baseman)

Drink because you are happy, but never because you are **miserable.**

G. K. Chesterton

Only a fool and passengers drink at sea.

Commander Alan Villiers

I must not mix champagne, whiskey and gin.
I must not mix champagne, whiskey and gin.
I must not mix champagne, whiskey and gin.
I must not mix champagne, whiskey and gin.
I must not mix champagne, whiskey and gin.
I must not mix champagne, whiskey and gin.
I must not mix champagne, whiskey and gin.
I must not mix champagne, whiskey and gin.
I must not mix champagne, whiskey and gin.
I must not mix champagne, whiskey and gin.
I must not mix champagne, whiskey and gin.
I must not mix champagne, whiskey and gin.
I must not mix champagne, whiskey and gin.
I must not mix champagne, whiskey and gin.
I must not mix champagne, whiskey and gin.
I must not mix champagne, whiskey and gin.

(repeated fifty times to fill his newspaper column after a long night)

Westbrook Pegler

There are two things that will be believed of any man whatsoever, and one of them is that he has taken to drink.

Booth Tarkington

I think a man ought to get drunk at least twice a year just on principle, so he won't let himself get snotty about it.

Raymond Chandler

31

If a man be discreet enough to take to hard drinking in his youth, before his

GENERAL EMPTINESS

is ascertained, his friends invariably credit him with a host of shining qualities which, we are given to understand, lie balked and frustrated by his own unfortunate weakness.

Agnes Repplier

One of the charms of drunkenness unquestionably lies in the deepening sense of reality and truth which is gained therein, In whatever light things may then appear to us, they seem more utterly what they are, more

'utterly utter'

than when we are sober.

William James

As your attorney, I advise you to drink heavily.
Hunter S. Thompson

There are two times when you can never tell what is going to happen.
One is when a man takes his first drink;
and the other is when a woman takes her latest.

O' Henry

It sets a man back in the esteem of people whose opinions are worth having.

Mark Twain
(on why he only got drunk once every three months)

32

Prudence must not be expected from a man who is never sober.

Cicero

Drunk: When a man feels *sophisticated* but can't pronouce it.

Irish Saying

James Cagney:
"A lush can always find a reason if he's thirsty. Listen.
If he's happy, he takes a couple of shots to celebrate his happiness.
Sad, he needs them to drown his sorrow.
Low, to pick him up, excited, to calm him down.
Sick, for his health and healthy, it can't hurt him ... a lush just can't lose."

'Come Fill The Cup'
(Warner Bros. 1951 screenplay)

Baths, wine and Venus bring decay to our bodies. But baths, wine and Venus make life worth living.

Latin Epitaph

33

"WHAT HAPPENS WHEN DRINK IS TAKEN"

I have taken more
out of alcohol
than alcohol has taken
out of me!
Winston Churchill

I owe a lot to booze!

Richard Burton

A man who has taken aboard two or three cocktails is less competent than he was before to steer a battleship down the Ambrose Channel, or to cut off a leg, or to draw up a deed of trust, or to conduct Bach's *B Minor Mass*, but he is immensely more competent to entertain a dinner party, or to admire a pretty girl, or to hear Bach's *B Minor Mass*. The harsh, useful things of the world, from pulling teeth to digging potatoes, are best done by men who are as starkly sober as so many convicts in the death-house, but the lovely useless things, the charming and exhilarating things, are best done by men with, as the phrase is, a few sheets in the wind. *Pithecanthropus erectus* was a teetotaler, but the angels, you may be sure, know what is proper at 5 p.m.

H. L. Mencken

*Quand mon verre est plein je le vide,
quand mon verre est vide je le plains.*
When my glass is full, I empty it,
and when my glass is empty, I pity it.

Richard O'Gorman

You think I'm
an asshole now?
You should've seen me
when I was drunk.

*John Cougar
Mellencamp*

I should never be allowed
out in private.
Randolph Churchill
(apologizing for his rudeness at a party)

To dispute with a
drunkard is to debate
with an empty house.

Publilius Syrus

34

"The Ten Stages Of Drunkeness"

1. Witty and Charming
2. Rich and Powerful
3. Benevolent
4. Clairvoyant
5. "Fuck Dinner"
6. Patriotic
7. "Crank Up the *Enola Gay*"
8. Witty Charming Part II
9. Invisible
10. Bulletproof

Dan Jenkins

Alcohol is the most powerful depressant of the central nervous system available in this country without a doctor's prescription. If it were being introduced now it would be a controlled drug.

Dr John Navard

The sway of alcohol over mankind is unquestionably due to its power to stimulate the mystical faculties of human nature, usually crushed to earth by the cold facts and dry criticisms of the sober hour. Sobriety diminishes, discriminates, and says No; drunkenness expands, unites and says Yes. It is in fact the great exciter of the Yes function in man. It brings its votary from the chill periphery of things to the radiant core. It makes him for the moment one with truth.

William James

I didn't know it at the time, but I had entered the drinking life. Drinking was part of being a man. Drinking was an integral part of sexuality, easing entrance to its dark and mysterious treasure chambers. Drinking was the sacramental binder of friendships. Drinking was the reward for work, the fuel of celebration, the consolation for death: It made me believe that dreams really could come true.

Pete Hamill

It's a cheat, she'd say. It's using the drink instead of forcing the painful choice.

Pete Hamill
(quoting Shirley MacLaine)

When I drink too much -
I get drunk.
When I get drunk -
I get tired.
When I get tired -
I go to sleep.
When I sleep -
I don't sin.
So - let's get drunk
and go to heaven!

sign in the 'Bonair Bar'

35

Wouldn't it be terrible if I quoted some reliable statistics which prove that more people are driven insane through religious hysteria than by drinking alcohol?

W. C. Fields

The only kind of spirit you see today in baseball is the kind you drink. *Johnny Mize*

I'll be honest: Beer and women hurt a lot of us.

Rod Frawley
(on why he and other Australian tennis players never lived up to expectations)

He that drinks fast, pays slow.

Benjamin Franklin

The cops picked me up on a street at 3:00 AM and fined me $500 for being drunk and $100 for being with the Phillies.

Bob Uecker

Ninety percent I'll spend on good times, women, and Irish whiskey. The other 10 percent I'll probably waste. *Tug McGraw*

Well, no man with two or three drinks in him is a tyrant. He may be foolish, but he is not cruel. He may be noisy, but he is also genial, tolerant, generous, and kind. My proposal would restore Christianity to the world. It would rescue mankind from moralists, pedants, and brutes.

H. L. Mencken

He doesn't drink, he doesn't smoke, he doesn't chew, he doesn't stay out late, and he still can't hit .250.

Casey Stengel
(on strait-laced Bobby Richardson)

In the order named, these are the hardest to control:

Wine, Women, and Song.

Franklin Pierce Adams

1st Lady:
"If I have another drink, I'm going to be feeling it."
2nd Lady:
"If I have another drink, I won't care who's feeling it."

Dorothy Parker

36

Porter: " ... drink, sir, is a great provoker of three things."
Macduff: "What three things does drink especially provoke?"
Porter: "Marry, sir, nose-painting, sleep, and urine. Lechery, sir, it provokes the desire, but it takes away the performance: Therefore much drink may be said to be an equivocator with lechery; it makes him, and it mars; it sets him on, and it takes him off; it persuades him, and disheartens him; makes him stand to, and not stand to: in conclusion, equivocates him in a sleep, and giving him the lie, leaves him."

William Shakespeare

Alcohol is a very necessary article. It enables Parliament to do things at eleven at night that no sane person would do at eleven in the morning. *George Bernard Shaw*

That is well said, John, an honest man, that is not quite sober, has nothing to fear. *Addisono*

When men began to drink - they burst into song, like birds,
When they drank more - they became strong as lions,
When they drank too much - they became stupid as asses.

14th century Swiss mural telling of a Greek legend

One old timer always said: "I never got into a fight when I was drinking, only when I was sober and knew what I was doing.

Because I was always so happy when I was drinking. I loved everybody and everybody seemed to love me. *Richard Erdoes*

In the meantime alcohol produces a delightful social atmosphere that nothing else can produce. *Arnold Bennett*

There is this to be said in favor of drinking, that it takes the drunkard first out of society, then out of the world. *Ralph Waldo Emerson*

Liquor is a Giant Killer and nobody who has not had to deal with the Giant many, many times has any right to speak against the

Giant Killer.

Ernest Hemingway

37

You couldn't disprove his story by the way he smelled.

Branch Rickey

(St. Louis Cardinals general manager, on the return of pitcher Flint Rhem, who claimed he'd been kidnapped and forced to consume large amounts of liquor while locked in a room)

Friendships are not always preserved in alcohol. *Wayside pulpit*

Who, after his wine, prates of war's hardships or of poverty? *Horace*

As you empty the bottles you refill them with your soul.

Gerard DeNerval

If all the tears and misery that are caused by alcohol could be rained down on this earth, I am sure that the whole of mankind would drown in the deluge.

Justice Lee

For liquor removed, temporarily, the innate suspicions of the mind; it paved the way for common thoughts, and feelings. For once, primitive man could look at foreign tribesman without a weapon in his hand. Indeed, at that epoch of evolution, when socialization hung in the balance, alcohol may have provided the social impulse which decided whether man was to form wider human groups or remain in that narrow tribal furrow.

Morris E. Chafetz

When a reformed drunkard gives advice you don't just hear it, you see it.

Dr Seldon Bacon

A couple of drinks might make a man democratic, but at the bottom of every glass thereafter lie superiority and aloofness.

Anon.

A **HOT DRINK** is as good as an overcoat.

Petronius

38

CHAPTER TWO

Pubs, Taverns & Saloons

DRINKING PLACES

A community life exists when one can go daily to a given location at a given time and see many of the people one knows!

P. Slater

The brewpub will do more to recreate a sense of community than any institution in modern day history. *Bill Metzger*

Here are your waters and your watering place. Drink and be whole again beyond confusion.

Robert Frost

One place I won't allow my players to drink is at the hotel where we're staying. That's where I do my drinking.

Hank Bauer
(Oakland A's manager)

The reason why I, and most others, usually turn out to enjoy meeting such creatures is simply and obviously the co-presence of drink. The human race has not devised any way of dissolving barriers, getting to know the other chap fast, breaking the ice, that is one-tenth as handy and efficient as letting you and the other chap, or chaps, cease to be totally sober at about the same rate in agreeable surroundings. *Kingsley Amis*

But aside from friends, there must also be a Place. I suppose that this is the **Great Good Place** that every man carries in his heart.

Pete Hamill

What marriage is to morality, a properly conducted licensed liquor traffic is to sobriety.

Mark Twain

For all of its fancy restaurants and cafes, there's not a single good neighborhood bar in Washington, a place where people of the area - young people, old people - congregate on a casual basis and talk about things over a beer or two.

Donald Kaul

NOBODY
drinks there anymore, the place is too busy.

Yogi Berra
(on why he and his friends didn't go to his restaurant)

40

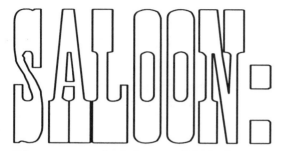

SALOON:

The poor man's club run with the intent to make the poor man poorer.
Frank McKinney Hubbard

The saloon has played an enormous part in America's psyche but the saloon as it was is vanishing. These places are significant to our history. They're where our grandparents stopped for one on the way home. *Alan D. Eames*

In a good saloon, anyone who has the price of a drink is as equal as anyone else - until he opens his mouth! *Mark Pollman*

Love it or hate it, the saloon in most of America's turbulent history played a vital and colorful role. Thru its swinging door passed some of the noblest of our countrymen - and some of the meanest and most despicable. Out of dramshops and taprooms came many of the highest ideals of freedom - and some of the worst emotions known to mortal man. Men gathered in them to try their fellows for crime, to whoop up rebellions against injustice, to listen to patriotic oratory and to settle political arguments. And men died in them by the tens of thousands, with their boots on. *Jim Marshall*

If it were not for saloons, where would lawyers go to recount their successes? *Allen D. Churchill*

Buddha says never to take anything in life too seriously - I say never take anything in saloons too seriously, unless you're about to get hit or lucky! *Mark Pollman*

If you pay attention in a saloon, sooner or later everyone will tell you exactly who they are - the sweethearts will be sweethearts, almost no matter what is done to them and the dummies will be dummies, no matter how much they try to cover up! *Mark Pollman*

I doted on the cool, refreshing scent of a good saloon on a hot summer day. *H. L. Mencken*

41

But every saloon very naturally became a political center - nowhere else, in most cities, was a workingman in working clothes welcome to stand around and talk politics. He could not afford to hire a hall; churches were not open to him; inclemencies of the weather and the '*move-along, now*' of the cops prevented street gatherings.

Jim Marshall

Saloon life radiated a bleary, beery charm immortalized late in song: "*Just mention 'saloon' and my cares fade away.*" A neighborhood saloon became the hub of a workingman's universe and he visited it daily, sometimes as frequently as morning noon, and night. A saloon gave a man a chance to air his political opinions; it gave him masculine privacy, a feeling of belonging, easy credit (despite curt notices on the wall to the contrary), escape from nagging household problems, and what's more, a free lunch.

Michael and Ariane Batterberry

(Saloons) resemble little theaters filled with challenging characters, dramatic vignettes, mysterious transactions, and diverse activities. The plots are usually tragic but there is comic relief. The bar structures and their settings within the city provide insight into urban life.

Taverns are frequently the oldest structures in a community and are often tenants of worn out hotels, homes, grocery stores and other old buildings.

Few (historians) have tried to weigh their detrimental and beneficial roles. Yet saloons can reveal much about urban America, about the lives of the poor and minorities, about class attitudes, about the commercial climate, about how politicians run a city, about crime and the underworld, about the unwritten history of cities.

If saloons fostered vice and political corruption, they also served as legitimate havens for the political, economic, and social activities of the urban poor, blue collar workers, racial minorities, and foreigners not welcome elsewhere.

Thomas J. Noel

Many left the office for the saloon next door, intending to have two before hopping the commuter train. However, the bar conversation was always so rich and revealing, the joy of jawing among one's confreres often lead to one more, and one more, and one more.

Jim Bishop (on newspaper people in New York)

42

What's more, the church was open about four hours every week and the saloon was open at least 108 hours and the city places were open 7 times 24, or 168 hours. Most of the churches harbored small groups of sedate men and women who were already saved and sanctified and ticketed for future rewards. The saloon gave boisterous welcome to every male adult, regardless of his private conduct, his clothes, his manners, his previous record or his ultimate destination. The saloon was the roostercrow of the spirit of democracy. It may have been the home of sodden indulgence and a training school for criminality, but it had a lot of enthusiastic comrades.

George Ade

Toot's will open again one block north. But that will be months, maybe a year, from now. In the meantime, as one New York paper noted in alarm, thousands of bums will be homeless.

Charles Champlin
(on the closing of Toots Shor's 51 West 51)

He is a tavern keeper in the old tradition. The strays of the night find their way to his bars, and so do the guys who make it big. Any place where Toots is has been a joint where men come to brag when they're proud and to fight the sorrow when it's bad.

Jimmy Cannon

He who has not been at a tavern knows not what a paradise it is.

Henry Wadsworth Longfellow

A tavern is the busy man's recreation, the idle man's business, the melancholy man's sanctuary, the stranger's welcome, the inn-of-courts man's entertainment, the scholar's kindness, and the citizen's courtesy.

Bishop Earle

A tavern is a house kept for those who are not housekeepers.

Chatfield

43

There's a touch of true magic in the word **tavern**. Let's go to a bar? - well, maybe. Let's go to a tavern? You can't say no.

The place is snug, the atmosphere and the decor masculine. The talk is small, but the dreams are big. The bartender's hands are busy, but the hands on the clock momentarily stand still. There is an unspoken fraternity to the place. A man may down his drink with a chuckle or a roar or a sigh, but that's his business and his alone.

Federic Birmingham

Without the tavern, the German proletariat has not only no social, but also no political life.

Karl Kautsky

We for a certainty
  are not the first
Have sat in taverns
  while the tempest hurled
Their hopeful plans
  to emptiness, and cursed
Whatever brute and black-
  guard made the world.

A. E. Housman

My respectable tavern is a quiet refuge and a hospital asylum from life and its cares!

H. L. Mencken

Many a man who thinks to have found a home discovers that he has merely opened a tavern for his friends.

Norman Douglas

... most of the noble notions of human freedom were invented, and plots for destroying tyranny hatched by men in taverns, their minds freed by drink from the necessity of worrying about commonplace troubles, so that lofty and ennobling conceptions of human dignity, liberty and comfort might be envisioned - as they frequently were.

Almost every drinker is familiar with the desire, after partaking of a few ounces of alcohol, to lead a better and fuller life, to escape from the dreadful round of money-making existence and destroy all men and evil forces leagued against the freedom of the common man. It was this desire, communally attained in pioneer saloons, that resulted almost every reform of government in America.

Jim Marshall

 In a good tavern, socializing rather than drinking is clearly most people's main occupation!

Tibor Scitovsky

As soon as I enter the door of a tavern, I experience an oblivion of care, and a freedom from solicitude: when I am seated, I find the master courteous, and the servants obsequious to my call; anxious to know and ready to supply my wants; wine there exhilarates my spirits, and prompts me to free conversation and an interchange of discourse with those whom I most love; I dogmatize and am contradicted, and in this conflict of opinion, I find delight.

Dr Samuel Johnson

For this my heart is set:
    When the hour is nigh me,
Let me in a tavern die,
    With a tankard by me.

Anon.

[the Restoration brought a revival of tavern life] - all ranks and conditions of people gathered there for every conceivable social purpose. It was a rendezvous, a business office, a postal address. Professional men and court officials were *'to be heard'* of at such and such a tavern. Debating societies and sportsmen used it as headquarters. It was a common meeting-ground, a club open to strangers, a centre of the life of the local community.

Ben Davis

He who has not been at a tavern knows not what a paradise it is.
O holy tavern! O miraculous tavern! - holy, because no carking cares are there, no weariness, nor pain;
and miraculous, because of the spits, which of themselves
turn round and round!

Aretino

My liquor's good,
my measure's just;
But, honest Sirs,
I will not trust.

Old tavern sign

Old Trust
is dead,
Bad Pay
killed him.

Old tavern sign

The gods who are most interested in the human race preside over the tavern. The tavern will compare favorably with the church. The church is the place where prayers and sermons are delivered but the tavern is where they take effect, and if the former are good the latter cannot be bad.

Henry David Thoreau

45

I desire to end my days
  in a tavern drinking,
May some Christian hold for me
  the glass when I am shrinking;
That the Cherubim may cry,
  when they see me sinking,
"God be merciful to a soul of
  this gentleman's way of thinking
Anon.

**IF YOU DRINK TO FORGET,
PLEASE PAY IN ADVANCE!**

Old tavern sign

BARS

To put it simply, all rituals in pubs
and bars issue from a collectively,
a *We,* while in coffeehouses the
I is central.

Wolfgang Schivelbusch

WHERE **NOT** TO GO

Rule # 1 Never go to a bar that serves umbrellas in your drink or colors your drink. Especially pink.

Rule # 2 Never go to a bar that has "Happy Hour". Nobody there ever is.

Rule # 3 Never go to a bar where the bartender has more problems than you do.

Rule # 4 Never go to a bar where you raise the average age of those inside by more than five years just by walking in.

Rule # 5 Although my favorite pubs are Irish pubs, never go to one on St. Paddy's day. It's amateur night and a good time to get a reservation at a Chinese restaurant.

Rule # 6 Never go to a bar where there is more than one bouncer unless you're expecting the trouble they are.

Rule # 7 Never go to a bar where they allow cell phones. A bar is a place of sanctity - check your self-importance at the door.

Rule # 8 Never go to a bar that does not ask you what brand you prefer but, instead, pours something called "Old Panther Piss" aged in the woods from the well underneath the counter.

Rule # 9 Never go to a bar that does not allow cigar smoking. A personal preference, granted, but you should tell anyone who complains "If it wasn't for twenty cigars a day, smoked by Winston Churchill, you'd be speaking German."

Rule # 10 Never drink and drive. The world needs designated drivers and where would they be without designated drunks sitting in the back seat getting sick all over themselves? They'd be out of work, that's where.

Bert Randolf Sugar

46

I never took the game home with me.
I always left it in some bar.
Bob Lemon
(Hall of Fame pitcher)

From personal experience everyone recognizes this unspoken obligation to participate in rounds of drinks regardless of whether he's in the mood or not, and even when he can't really afford it. Not to go along with it would be to lose face.

Yet this sort of obligation holds true only in bars, pubs and saloons, and only in connection with alcoholic drinks. The idea of such a thing happening in a restaurant would be absurd. What is natural in a bar is meaningless on the outside.
Wolfgang Schivelbusch

How much of our literature, our political life, our friendships and love affairs, depend on being able to talk peacefully in a bar!

John Wain

Human beings are at their best in bars.
Alex Waugh

I must have.
I remember the bar across the street.
Rod Laver
(on whether he played a certain tournament in New Jersey)

HARVARD UNIVERSITY
was pleasantly and conveniently situated in the barroom of Parker's.
Artemus Ward

Public drinking places are 'open regions': those who are present, acquainted or not, have the right to engage others in conversational interaction and the duty to accept the overtures of sociability proffered to them. While many, and perhaps the majority, of conventional settings customarily limit the extent of contact among strangers, sociability is the general rule in the public drinking places. Although the bar is typically populated primarily by strangers, interaction is available to all those who choose to enter. The physical door through which one enters a drinking establishment is a symbolic door as well, for those who come through it declare by entering that unless they put forth evidence to the contrary, they will be open for conversation with unacquainted others for the duration of their stay. Whatever their age, sex, or apparent position, their biographical blemishes or physical stigmas, all who enter are immediately vested with the status of an open person, open both in having the right to make contact with the others present and in the general obligation of being open to others who may contact them.

American sociological study

The old days when father spent his evenings at Cassidy's bar with the rest of the boys are gone, and probably gone forever, Cassidy may still be in the business at the old stand and father may still go down there of evenings, but since Prohibition, mother goes down with him.

Elmer Davis

I go from stool to stool in singles bars hoping to get lucky, but there's never any gum under any of them.

Emo Phillips

Across the Street and Into the Bar.

E. B. White

(Title of a satire on Ernest Hemingway)

These smaller bars really took the place of the American living room. No one ever entertained at home, first because French housing laws do not permit any noise after ten o'clock, and secondly because it was so much more economical to meet your friends in a bar where each paid for his own drink. In this manner there was no bother of giving invitations or keeping dates. Knowing, as most Quarterites did, several hundred other Montparnessians, you were certain to encounter at least three or four congenial souls no matter what bar you visited!

Jimmie Charters

Pubs

When I go to Heaven I want to be in an English pub, which has been stocked by an American landlord with a Rubenesque barmaid in floury skin and black satin, and I will be drinking cold Australian beer.

Gareth Powell

[The Pub] was a revolutionary invention [and] immediately began to erode the whole traditional image of the hotel as a house.

Mark Girouard

The word **'pub'** is the most compressed piece of shorthand in the world. The village pub is a drinking house, a parish parliament, and a club rolled into one.

Timothy Finn

Indeed one of the advantages of a pub over a club is precisely that it is 'open to strangers' - one is not cut off from the life of the town. Absolutely anybody *may* come in.

Ben Davis

It was a swing door.
You can't bang a pub door.
The pubs know a lot,
almost as much as the churches.
They've got a tradition.

Joyce Carey

The Pub, some call it *'The Greatest Of All English Inventions'*. Here great battles have been waged, truces signed, friendships sealed. The pub, isn't just a place to drink dark beer, it's the very soul of England - across the nation, it's the clubhouse of almost every village.

John Hemingway

They spoke of Progress spring round,
Of Light and Mrs. Humphrey Ward-
It is not true to say I frowned,
Or ran about the room and roared;
I might have simply sat and snored -
And said "I feel a little bored.
Will someone take me to a pub?"

G. K. Chesterton

The function of the pub is company, human nearness, ... snugness not smugness.

Nikolaus Pevsner

49

A pub is a poor man's

UNIVERSITY

Sign in *The Humbert Inn,* Castlebar, County Mayo

The keynote of the public house and its true purpose in life is Christian Charity.
H. P. Maskell and E. W. Gregory

A pub needs its trace-element of vulgarity to keep it lusty.
John Piper

However, when they choose to reject anyone who wears no tie, or his hair too long, or who speaks with a *posh* accent, the pub at once becomes something less than a pub.
Ben Davis

[The pub] is the haunt of the common man ... the citizen who whatever his rank or position meets other citizens as equals at the bar.
Leslie Forse

IRISH PUBS

We had gone out there to pass the beautiful day of high summer like true Irishmen - locked in the dark Snug of a public house.
Brendan Behan

Dublin's pubs are temples of good conversation.
Rick Steves

The beauty of it is that this is where the pace changes in the day. For it be true in the Irish pub - it's like going to the parlor of a country. You're always made welcome - you can never be alone in an Irish pub.

It's also the place where the problems of the world are solved. You know that we are able to solve problems like the American space race, US - Soviet relationships, stuff like that.
A Day in the Life of Ireland

Dublin is the great mother of all Irish pubs. When you first come to Dublin you can almost believe that the town was invented as an excuse for the creation of pubs. There is a pub for every occasion, from funeral to dart contest, and for every kind of person, from barrister to fisherman. There are even pubs that mix all these elements together. A word of warning: It *is* possible to so enjoy pub-crawling in Dublin that you endlessly postpone departure.
Sybil Taylor

When I die I want to decompose in a barrel of porter and have it served in all the pubs in Dublin. I wonder would they know it was me.
J. P. Donleavy

50

INNS

It's better to sit in the inn thinking about church than to sit in the church thinking about the inn.
Danish saying

When you have lost your inns, drown your empty selves, for you will have lost the last of England.
Hilaire Belloc

Whoe'er has travell'd life's dull round,
  Where'er his stages may have been,
May sigh to think he still has found
  The warmest welcome at an inn.

    'Tis here with boundless power I reign,
      And every health which I begin,
    Coverts dull port to bright champagne;
      For Freedom crowns it, at an inn ...
And now once more I shape my way
  Through rain or shine, through thick or thin,
Secure to meet, at the close of day,
  With kind reception at an inn.
William Shenstone

CLUBS & NIGHTCLUBS

You really grow up fast in a nightclub.
Wayne Newton

Most clubs have the atmosphere of a Duke's house with the Duke lying dead upstairs.
Douglas Sutherland

It is easier for a man to be loyal to his club than to his planet; the by-laws are shorter, and he is personally acquainted with the other members.
E. B. White

At Dirty Dick's and Sloppy Joe's
  We drank our liquor straight,
Some went upstairs with Margery,
  And some, alas, with Kate.
Wystan Hugh Auden

I worked in a night-club that had midget waiters - to make the drinks look bigger!
Milton Berle

A night club is a place where people with nothing to remember go to forget.
Grove Patterson

A night club is a saloon with an orchestra.
Matthew Weinstock

51

C U S T O M E R S

Rules of Conduct For Those Who Drink In Public:

1. Never Stand next to Anyone in a Bar that is Drinking Red Wine.
2. Expect Constant Interruptions if You try to Read a Newspaper.
3. Avoid ANYONE Who asks You to Name the Seven Dwarfs, the Members of the Supreme Court, or the National League MVP in '58.
4. NEVER Slam the Bar Dice (or Your Change for that matter).
5. Always TIP SOFT, not to be confused with LIGHT!
6. GO SLOW, the Opposite Sex Always Looks Better at Closing Time.
7. Drinks Taste Progressively Better as the Evening wears on.
8. The Bartender is ALWAYS Right.
9. NEVER Talk about Anyone you know when They go to the Restroom. Sound in a Bar Travels in Straight Lines to the Toilets.
10. Always Edge into the Mirror in the Morning.

sign at the Washington Square Bar & Grill, San Francisco, CA

A perfect customer is one who knows what he wants to drink and orders it; keeps himself entertained; and tips when he leaves.

Bartender at the North Star Hotel, Minneapolis

Out drinking with two fellow poets, Anne Sexton parked in a "Loading Only Zone." "It's O.K.," she told her companions, "we're only going to get loaded."

Regulars do not go home and dress up. Rather, they come as they are! *Ray Oldenburg*

A tourist asked the proprietor of an inn in the Highlands if they played any games in his place. "Games," said the innkeeper scornfully, "na, na, sir, my customers are none of your light-headed kind. They take drinkin' seriously here." *Anon.*

A man may surely be allowed to take a glass of wine by his own fireside. *Richard Brinsley Sheridan*
(on being encountered drinking a glass of wine in the street, while watching his theater, the Drury Lane, burn down)

CHAPTER THREE

Bartenders, Waitresses, & Tipping

The Man Behind The Bar

He deserves a hero's medal for the many lives he's saved,
  And upon the Role of Honour his name should be engraved.
He deserves a lot of credit for the way he stands the strain.
  For the yarns he has to swallow would drive most of us insane.

He must pay the highest license, he must pay the highest rent.
  He must battle with his Bank and pay his ten percent.
And when it comes to paying bills, he's always on the spot.
  He pays for what he sells, whether you pay him or not.

And when you walk into his Bar, he'll greet you with a smile.
Be you a workman dressed in overalls or a banker dressed in style
If you're Irish, English, Scotch or Welsh, it doesn't matter what.
He'll treat you like a gentleman, unless you prove you're not.

Yet the clergy in the pulpit and the preacher in the hall
  Will assure him that the churches are against him one and all.
But when the churches plan to hold a ballot or bazaar,
  They start by selling tickets to the man behind the Bar.

When he retires, a job well done, to await six feet of soil,
  Discards his coat and apron, no more on earth to toil.
As Saint Peter sees him coming, he will leave those gates ajar,
  For he knows he had his Hell on Earth.
The Man Behind The Bar.   *Anon.*

Bartending Styles

I feel I have over a thousand friends, and any man considers himself lucky to have five or six friends, but a saloonkeeper has the opportunity to meet a thousand and keep having them as friends.

Toots Shor

The leader-writer in a great Northern daily said on the morning after King Edward died that if he had not been a king he would have been the best type of sporting publican.

James Agate

Possibly the first requirement in a barmaid or barman is that he/she should enjoy her/his work. An equable temperament is basic to the task. Too much hearty laughter can be as badly out of place as a morose countenance, and a skillful operator will judge and adjust himself to the mood of his customers, conversing with the talkative and respecting the privacy of the introspective. Worst of all bar people is the avid reader, who, at a slack time, returns to his paperback or comic after serving a lone customer. Attributes which are (or should be) taken for granted are speed, efficiency and a quick eye for an empty glass: but none of these are of much use if they are accompanied by a stern look on a straight face. Nor should it be forgotten that a genial rudeness is always preferable to a false deference.

Ben Davis

The Bartender Knows

He knows all our Sorrows,
  He knows all our Joys,
He knows all the Girls who are chasing the Boys.

He knows all our Troubles,
  He knows all our Strife,
He knows every Man who ducks out from his Wife.

If Bartender told all he knows,
  He would turn our Friends into bitterest Foes;
He would start forth a Story, which gaining in Force,
  Would cause all our Wives to sue for Divorce;

He would get all our Homes mixed up in a Fight,
  He would turn all our bright Days
Into Sorrowing Nights;

In fact He would keep the town in a Stew,
  If he told One-Tenth of All that He knew.

So when out on a Party,
  And from Home you Steal,
Drop in for a Drink,
  The Bartender won't Squeal.

Anon.

55

Dudley, the bartender, was a man of few words, but when he did speak he was very funny. One night a woman said to him, "Dudley, don't you ever smile?" He replied, "Delivering the sacrament is no joke, madam."

There are only three Rules to running a good saloon:

#1. The Bartender is always right!
#2. See Rule number 1.
#3. See Rule number 2.

Mark Pollman

Talk to me, honey.
Make believe I'm
your bartender!

Leopold Fetchner

Better to pay the tavernkeeper than the druggist.

Spanish proverb

Through booze I met two chief justices, fifty world champs, six presidents and DiMaggio and Babe Ruth.

Toots Shor

My last hope was to become a bartender. That trade still glittered and smoked for me with the flames of Hell. So, I made myself as agreeable to the head bartender of the Harbor as I knew how. At last we got very confidential - and then what did he do but begin to deliver beery lectures on Bach and Handel, Beethoven and Wagner! One night he laid off and took me to a concert! The band played the grand piece called *The Eroica*. After the concert the head bartender cried into his beer as he told me how he had always wanted to play the flute in the orchestra ... He went to moaning and swearing in German; and I listened to him and felt sick as I began to realize that, actually, bartending was just a common job ... Certainly a man wasn't wicked who cried because he couldn't play a flute ... The last hope was gone. So I gave up at last and took the saloon for what it actually was: a handsome, comfortable, fine-smelling place, where a man could drink liquors .. and where the best in him would be brought forth and paraded for the inspiration and instruction of his fellow man.

James Stevens

Bartenders & Control

(In the bar) the boss is a potentate. What he says goes. In England, the publican is called 'Governor', and not without reason. By custom and tradition, he is the best man in the house. He sets the tone. Behind every good saloon, you will find a good man ... These lads are social leaders. By his example and his graces, he teaches manners to the less worldly, whom he appears to service.

Charles McCabe

My customers may not always be right, But they are always first!

Tom Burnham

Famous last words: "That's the last time I tell a bartender anything." *Anon.*

[The tavern keeper] is confidante and psychologist in one; defender of the weak and peer of the strong; a listener of infinite patience; and when opportunity offers, a conversationalist of ringing eloquence.

The very motion of his hands and measured eye - sure, decisive and muscular - often serves as a show in itself for the sedentary types on the other side of the bar who admire a man of action, especially when they see one bent on such a saving errand.

Frederic Birmingham

Who Becomes A Bartender.

There are strings in the human heart which must never be sounded by another, and drinks that I make myself are those strings in mine.

Charles Dickens

I look like somebody's bartender.

Dean Rusk

I never said all Democrats were saloonkeepers. What I said was that all saloonkeepers were Democrats.

Horace Greeley

Bartenders, cocktail waitresses, cops and hospital emergency-room people know when a moon is really full.

Mark Pollman

The cheapest and easiest way to become an influential man and be looked up to by the community at large, was to stand behind a bar, wear a cluster diamond pin, and sell whiskey. I am not sure but the saloonkeeper held a shade higher rank than any other member of society. His opinion had weight. It was a privilege to say how elections should go. No great movement could succeed without the countenance and direction of the saloonkeeper. It was a high favor when the chief saloonkeeper consented to serve in the legislature or the board of alderman.

Mark Twain

57

Do not allow children to mix drinks. It is unseemly and they use too much vermouth!
Fran Lebowitz

What's the difference between a bartender and a stagecoach driver? - A stagecoach driver only has to look at six of them at a time.
Anon.

Englishman in a Dublin pub: "Bartender, give me another pint of Guiness and a bit more subservience, please!".
Anon.

Any man with a bottle in each hand can't be all bad.
a customer's reflection on bartenders

The most notorious of these amusements, thrown by the new money of M. et Mme. Natanson, would have preempted the first cocktail parties by nearly a decade, had it not started after eight. Toulouse-Lautrec tended bar that night - which lasted till dawn - standing chin-high before a sign that read in English *"Don't Speak To The Man At The Wheel."*

He concocted, at his estimate, two thousand cocktails, among them elaborate, layered drinks of red, green and yellow liqueurs, surreal inventions of sardines and gin set alight in long silver dishes.

Jill Spalding

58

Waitresses Barmaids

Not turning taps, but pulling pumps,
give barmaids splendid busts and rumps.

The New Statesman

A barmaid is what the boys in the backroom
will have.

L. L. Levinson

And fifteen arms went around her waist,
(And then men ask, 'Are barmaids chaste?').

John Masefield

On the chest of a barmaid in Sale
Were tattooed the prices of ale,
   And on her behind,
   For the sake of the blind,
was the same information in Braille.

Anon.

Anon. Sign

My pulpit is an alehouse bench,
   Whereon I sit so jolly;
A smiling rosy country wench,
   My saint and patron holy.
I kiss her cheek so red and sleek,
   I press her ringlets wavy,
And in her willing ear I speak,
   A most religious *Ave.*

William Makepeace Thackery

With breast and buttocks firm as trees
The barmaid-waitress blooms and sways,
And drinking timberman appraise
How thighs grow upwards from the knees,
And tractor drivers' glances state
That doors they know of have no locks,
And love wears deftly zippered frocks.
When sudden spring and moonlight mate.
   And shearers ask for leg and tart;
   No matter what the table lacks,
   These come to them as midnight snacks
   Kept hot and served with lusty art.

Colin Thiele

59

Tips & Tipping

A tip is a small sum of money you give to someone because you are afraid he wouldn't like not being paid for something you haven't asked him to do.

Ann Ceasar

"What is the difference between valor and discretion?"
"Well, to drink in here without tipping would be valor."
"I see."
"And to drink in another pub next would be discretion."

Anon.

Tips are wages paid to other people's hired help.

Anon.

I like to pay postilions and waiters rather more liberally than perhaps is right. I hate grumbling and sour faces; and the whole saving will not exceed a guinea or two for being cursed and damned from Dan to Beersheba.

Sir Walter Scott

It is wise to tip well on the way up in case you meet the same dreary, greedy cunts on the way down.

P. V. Taylor

The difference between a Scotchman and a canoe: a canoe tips.

Leopold Fetchner

Waiter (to customer):
"That fine line between gracious attendance and fawning obsequiousness - tell me, sir, how close did I come?"

William Hamilton

Lord Rothschild left what he considered to be an adequate tip. The waiter responded disdainfully, "Your lordship's son always gives me a good deal more than this." "I daresay he does," retorted Rothschild, "But you see he has a rich father, I haven't."

Anon.

Whin I give a tip 'tis not because I want to but because I'm afraid iv what th' waiter'll think.

Finley Peter Dunne

60

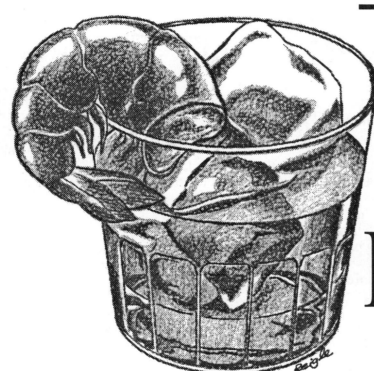

CHAPTER FOUR

Dining, Drinking & Parties

Reasons For Liquor With Food

Why does man kill? Man kills for food. And not only for food - frequently, there must be a beverage.

Woody Allen

Wine is meant to be with food - that's the point of it.

Julia Child

Besides being wonderful to drink with food, wines used delicately can add new enjoyment to the preparation of food. This centuries-old supplement to meals has played an important role in civilization and will continue to. The learning process can be exciting for any person - and who among us doesn't want to get a little more stimulation out of life.?

James A. Hart

A rich meal without wine is like an expensive automobile equipped with hard rubber tires.

Roy Louis Alciatore

In Bordeaux, as in the rest of France, the marriage of food and wine is celebrating hundreds of years of happiness. If there is relatively little thrill or experimentation, well, that's the way it often is with successful long-term marriage. But there's plenty of the ease, comfort and pleasure of partners content with each other.

Florence Fabricant

I told him ... that we ate when we were not hungry and drank without the provocation of thirst.

Jonathan Swift

62

DINNER

If wine were made accessible to all classes in this country, temperance societies would soon be superfluous. For when the frugal meal of our humble labourer and artizan is cheered (as elsewhere) by a wholesome and invigorating beverage, drunkenness will gradually disappear.

"Wine In Relation To Temperance"

Indeed beer has been the only thing that has permitted generations of Englishmen to endure the cooking of English cooks without murdering them.

Anon.

Only Irish coffee provides in a single glass all four essential food groups: Alcohol, caffeine, sugar and fat.

Alex Levine

If the soup had been as hot as the claret, if the claret had been as old as the bird, and if the bird's breasts had been as full as the waitress's, it would have been a very good dinner.

Anon.

Dinner at the Huntercombes' possessed only two dramatic features - the wine as a farce and the food a tragedy.

☺☹ *Anthony Powell*

Red Bordeaux is like the lawful wife: an excellent beverage that goes with every dish and enables one to enjoy one's food. But now and then a man wants a change.

Frank Harris

For a gourmet wine is not a drink but a condiment, provided that your host has chosen it correctly.

Edouard DePomiane

The object of dinner is not to eat and drink, but to join in merrymaking and make lots of noise. For that reason, he who drinks half drinks best.

Lin Yutang

63

Food With Liquor

How simple and frugal a thing is
happiness: a glass of wine, a roasted
chestnut, a wretched little brazier,
the sound of the sea … All that is
required to feel that here and now
happiness is a simple, frugal heart.

Nikos Kazantzakis

At last I've seduced the *au pair*
With some steak and a chocolate eclair,
  Some peas and some chips,
  Three Miracle Whips,
And a carafe of vin ordinaire.

Cyril Ray

I no longer prepare Food or Drink
with more than one Ingredient.

Cyra McFadden

Drink a glass of wine after your soup
and you steal a ruble from the doctor.

Russian proverb

It was my Uncle George who discovered
that alcohol was a food well in advance of
modern medical thought.

P. G. Wodehouse

Russians will consume marinated mush-
rooms and vodka, salted herring and
vodka, smoked salmon and vodka, salami
and vodka, caviar on brown bread and
vodka, pickled cucumbers and vodka,
cold tongue and vodka, red beet salad
and vodka, scallions and vodka -
anything and everything and vodka.

Hedrick Smith

Someone is putting brandy
in your bonbons,
Grand Marnier
in your breakfast,
Kahlua in your ice cream,
Scotch in your mustard
and Wild Turkey in your cake.

Marian Burros

A heavy drinker was
offered grapes at dessert.
"No thank you," he said,
pushing the dish away
from him, "I am not in
the habit of taking my
wine in the form of pills."

Brillat-Savarin

It's all right
Arthur, the
white wine
came up with
the fish.

*Herman
Mankiewicz*
*American
screenwriter
(after vomiting
at the table of
stuffy producer
Arthur Hornblow)*

64

Types of Parties

The Crucifixion was just one of those parties that got out of hand.
Lenny Bruce

It was one of those parties where you cough twice before you speak and then decide not to say it after all.
P. G. Wodehouse

Have you ever been at a party when you were too tired to listen and too courteous to leave?
Herbert V. Prochnow Sr.

When the hostess of a party asked if he was enjoying himself, **George Bernard Shaw** replied, "Certainly, there is nothing else here to enjoy."

THE COCKTAIL PARTY

A cocktail party is what you call it when you invite everyone you know to come to your house at six p.m., put cigarettes out on your rug, and leave at eight to go somewhere interesting for dinner without inviting you. Cocktail parties are very much on their way out among rug-owning, hungry, snubbed people.
P. J. O'Rourke

The Cocktail Party - as the name itself indicated - was originally invented by dogs. They are simply bottom sniffings raised to the rank of formal ceremonies.
Lawrence Durrell

The cocktail party - a device for paying off obligations to people you don't want to invite to dinner.
Charles Merril Smith

THE COCKTAIL PARTY - is a device either for getting rid of social obligations hurriedly en masse or for making overtures toward more serious social relationships, as in the etiquette of whoring.
Brooks Atkinson

There must be some good in the cocktail party to account for its immense vogue among otherwise sane people.
Evelyn Waugh

A gathering held to enable forty people to talk about themselves at the same time. The man who remains after the liquor is gone is the host.
Fred Allen   (on Cocktail Parties)

65

After the first hour a large cocktail party sounds like a zoo at feeding time.
Herbert V. Prochnow, Sr

The cocktail party remains a vital Washington institution, the official intelligence system.
Barbara Howar

HOSTS & HOSTESSES

The ice of her
Ladyship's manners,
The ice of his
Lordship's champagne.
W. M. Praed

The great
Should be as large in liquor
as in love.
E. A. Robinson

The hostess must be like a duck - calm and unruffled on the surface, and paddling like hell underneath.
Anon.

He's the kind of guy who would throw a beer party and then lock the bathroom door on you.
George Raveling
(on Bobby Knight)

When her guests were awash with champagne and gin,
She was recklessly sober, as sharp as a pin.
William Plomer

You have the right to drink badly, you never have the right to make others do so.
Louis Forest

There have been many friends with simple tables and modest cellars, about whom it can be said that the soft extractive note of an aged cork being withdrawn has been the true sound of a man opening his heart.
William Samuel Benwell

I accept refreshments from any hands, however lowly.
W. S. Gilbert

Strong drink is intended to be used in entertaining guests: such employment of it is what Heaven has prescribed.
"The Shoo-king"

To know how to drink wine belongs only to a cultivated taste: to know how to tempt guests to indulge in it with pleasure belongs only to the host gifted with rare tact and artistic discrimination.
The Cocktail Book
'A Sideboard Manual for Gentlemen'

Consider yourselves introduced, because I only remember one of your names, and that wouldn't be fair to the other.
Sir Herbert Beerbohm Tree

66

A host is like a general: it takes a mishap to reveal his genius.
Horace

The best parties are given by people who can't afford them.
Elsa Maxwell

The greater the kindness of my host, the greater my anxiety not to impose on it.
Voltaire

In good company, you need not ask who is the master of the feast. The man who sits in the lowest place, and who is always industrious in helping everyone, is certainly the man.
David Hume

Giving parties is a trivial avocation, but it pays the dues for my union card in humanity.
Elsa Maxwell

GUESTS & HOW TO BE ONE

The truly free man is he who refuses an invitation to dinner without giving any reason for it.
Jules Renard

First I want a woman guest to be beautiful. Second, I want her to be beautifully dressed. Third, I demand animation and vivacity. Fourth, not too many brains. Brains are always awkward at a gay and festive party.
Elsa Maxwell

Three bowls only do I mix for the temperate:
one to health, which they empty first,
the second to love and pleasure,
the third to sleep. When this is drunk up
the wise guests go home.   *Ebulus*

Remember, it is your prerogative to drink or not. A firm "No, thank you" or "Plain soda, please" will not automatically label you a party pooper and may win added respect. Remember Bernard Baruch's advice, "Those who mind don't matter, and those who matter don't mind."
Jane E. Brody

While at a literary cocktail party, Maxwell Perkins argued that no one attending such affairs ever really listened to what anyone else had to say. To prove his point he said on shaking his hostess' hand in the midst of the crowded room, "I'm sorry I'm late, but it took me longer to strangle my aunt then I expected." "Yes, indeed," his hostess replied. "I'm so happy you can come."

67

One does not leave a convivial party before closing time.

Winston Churchill

No one walks into a party without having a far better party going on inside his head. Every party is going to be that party until we get there. So the key to the boredom and tension at parties is that no one wants to be at the party he's missing.

Jules Feiffer

Don't think it has been charming, because it hasn't.

Margot Asquith

The Life and Soul, the man who will never go home while there is one man, woman or glass of anything not yet drunk.

Katherine Whitehorn

"Have some wine," the March Hare said in an encouraging tone. Alice looked all around the table, but there was nothing on it but tea. "I don't see any wine," she remarked. "There isn't any," said the March Hare. "Then it wasn't very civil of you to offer it," said Alice angrily.

Lewis Carroll

A gentleman having to some of the usual arguments for drinking added this: *"You know Sir, drinking drives away care, and makes us forget whatever is disagreeable. Would not you allow a man to drink for that reason?"* Dr Samuel Johnson: *"Yes, Sir, if he sat next to you."*

Anon.

Dorothy Parker was asked to leave *William Randolph Hearst's* palatial San Simeon, either for drinking or for sleeping with another guest. Thinking this hypocritical, since Hearst drank and loved there with his mistress, act-

ress Marion Davies, she wrote the following in the visitor's book on leaving:
Upon my honor,
I saw a Madonna
Standing in a niche,
Above the door
Of the famous whore
Of a prominent son of a bitch.

Anon.

Rumour has it that the final rupture between Beau Brummel and the Prince of Wales came about as a result of the following incident:
The Beau was bidden to a party of men only at Carlton House and the usual hard drinking began after the withdrawal of the servants. Brummel had the place of honor next to the Prince. The Prince turned suddenly towards his favorite, and, without a word, threw a glass of wine into his face. The Beau, immediately recovering his self-possession, lifted his own glass and flung the contents into the face of his neighbor at the other side, with the words, "The Prince's toast; pass it around."

W. B. Boulter

Cocktails &
Concoctions

REASONS FOR DRINKING COCKTAILS

There is something about an old-fashioned
  That kindles a cardiac glow;
It is soothing and soft and impassioned
  As a lyric by Swinburne or Poe.

There is something about an old-fashioned
  When dusk has enveloped the sky,
And it may be the ice,
  Or the pineapple slice,
But I strongly suspect it's the rye.

Ogden Nash

That faint but sensitive
ENTERIC EXPECTANCY
that suggests the
desirability of a cocktail.

Christopher Morley

A Frenchman drinks his native wine,
A German drinks his beer;
An Englishman his 'alf and 'alf,
Because it brings good cheer.
The Scotchman drinks
  his whisky straight
Because it brings on dizziness;
An American has no choice at all -
He drinks the whole damn business.

Anon.

The cocktail epoch.
COCKTAILS!
They are of all colors.
They contain something of everything.
No, I do not merely mean the cocktails
that one drinks. They are symbolic of
the rest. The modern society woman
is a cocktail. She is a bright mixture.
Society itself is a bright mixture.
You can blend people of all tastes and
classes. The cocktail epoch!

Kees van Dongen (Dutch artist in Paris)

When evening quickens in the
street, comes a pause in the day's
occupation that is known as the
cocktail hour. It marks the lifeward turn. The heart wakens
from coma and its dyspnea ends.
Its strengthening pulse is to
cross over into the campground,
to believe that the world has not
been altogether lost or, if lost,
then not altogether in vain.

Bernard De Voto

There is no doubt that Jeeve's
pick-me-up will produce
immediate results in anything
short of an Egyptian mummy.

P. G. Wodehouse

The future of American thought,
poetry, and religion - the future of
the American world - is intimately
interwoven with whiskey sours!

Delmore Schwartz

A properly mixed cocktail can be delightful and potent, able to revive a corpse or a jaded appetite. It has a complex appeal, it dispenses moods, being the subtle result of the collaboration of the scientist and the poet - that is, the barman. And we must admit that cocktails remain the most romantic expression of modern life, of post-war civilization.

X. M. Boulestin

She was rather like one of those innocent-tasting American drinks which creep into your system so that, before you know what you're doing, you're starting out to reform the world by force if necessary, and pausing on your way to tell the large man in the corner that, if he looks at you like that, you will knock his head off.

P. G. Wodehouse

Cocktails are society's most enduring invention!

Elsa Maxwell

A cocktail is to a glass of wine as rape is to love.

Paul Claudel

MARTINIS

The reason that I don't drink Martinis is that if I drink Martinis I drink a lot of Martinis and after drinking a lot of Martinis - I get very drunk and very sloppy. But when I get very drunk - I also get very horny, but I'm so sloppy that I can't do anything about being very horny - so then I get very mean - so, now, I just don't drink Martinis and life is better.

Mark Pollman

Generally, the martini signifies absolute decadence. Specifically it means a bitter, medicinal - tasting beverage. It stands for everything from phony bourgeois values and social snobbery to jaded alcoholism and latent masochism.

James Villas

71

Martinis are like a woman's breast - one's not enough and three's too many, unless it's in the back for dancing!

Mark Pollman

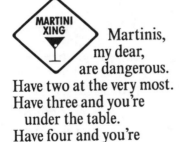 Martinis, my dear, are dangerous. Have two at the very most. Have three and you're under the table. Have four and you're under the host.

Dorothy Parker

I am prepared to believe that a dry martini slightly impairs the palate, but think what it does for the soul.

Alec Waugh

The Martini is America's supreme gift to the world. ... With the Martini we reach a fine and noble art ... You can no more keep a martini in the refrigerator than you can keep a kiss there. The proper union of gin and vermouth is a great and sudden glory; it is one of the happiest marriages on earth and one of the shortest-lived. The fragile tie of ecstasy is broken in a few minutes, and thereafter there can be no remarriage. The beforehander has not understood that what is left, though it was once a martini, can never be one again. He has sinned as seriously as the man who leaves some in a pitcher to drown.

Bernard De Voto

The Martini is nicknamed 'the silver bullet' because of its supposedly lethal properties. This nickname also seems to contain a hint of the Martini's sensitivity. Although this cocktail is a lethal bullet, it is made of silver, not some base metal.

Lowell Edmunds

 "I think it's a fine name," said Bond. An idea struck him. "Can I borrow it?" He explained about the special martini he had invented, and his search for a name for it. "The Vesper," he said, "It sounds very appropriate to the violet hour when my cocktail will now be drunk all over the world. Can I have it?"

Just a moment. Three measures of Gordon's, one of vodka, half a measure of Kina Lillet. Shake it very well until it's ice-cold, then add a large thin slice of lemon-peel. Got it?"

'Casino Royale' (the girl: Vesper Lynd)

Ian Fleming

72

Two men driving down a street one day noticed a pair of dogs copulating. One man said to the other, "Gee, I wish I could prevail upon my wife to do it that way." The other said, "That's easy. Just give her three Martinis and she'll do it any way you want." The man said, "Well, maybe I should try that." About a week later, they met again and the man who had given the advice asked, "Well, did you try the Martinis? How did you get along?" The man replied, "Well, I got along very well, but you were way off on your count - I had to give her five Martinis just to get her out on the front lawn."

Anon.

PARTICULARLY NAMED CONCOCTIONS

The first known reference to the cocktail:

[Question]:

Sir, I observe in your paper of the 6th inst., in the account of a democratic candidate for a seat in the Legislature, marked under in the head of Loss, 25 do., 'cocktail'.

Will you be so obliging as to inform me what is meant by this species of refreshment? I have heard of a *jorum*, of *phlegm cutter* and *fog cutter*, of *wetting the whistle* and *moistening the clay*, of a *fillip*, a *spur in the head, quenching a spark in the throat*, of *flip*, etc., but never in my life, though I have lived a good many years, did I hear of cocktail before. Is it peculiar to a part of this country? Or is it a late invention?

Is the name expressive of the effect which the drink has on a particular part of the body? Or does it signify that the Democrats who make the potion are turned topsy turvy, and have their heads where their tails are?

[Editor's answer]:

Cocktail is a stimulating liquor, composed of spirits of any kind, sugar, water and bitters - it is vulgarly called bittered sling and is supposed to be an excellent engineering potion, inasmuch as it renders the heart stout and bold, at the same time that it fuddles the head. It is said also, to be of great use to a Democratic candidate: because, a person having swallowed a glass of it, is ready to swallow anything else.

The Balance and
Columbian Repository

Hudson, NY, May 13, 1806

73

There are many legends regarding the origin of the term cocktail. Perhaps the most popular one relates to Betsy's Tavern, which was a meeting place for French and American officers of Washington's army in 1779. There, the Irish barmaid - Betsy Flanagan - decorated her special drinks with the feathers from a cock's tail and it is said that one of the Frenchmen calling for a toast exclaimed *vive le cocktail*, after which all of Betsy's concoctions were called cocktails.

Another is that a chemist in New Orleans entertained his friends with mixed drinks which he served in double-ended egg cups, *coquetiers,* which the Amer- turned into 'cockters' and, thereafter, cocktail.

There is also the legend of American origin, of a barkeeper who used a small natural root known as *cola de tallo*, from its shape, which was translated as cock's tail.

Peter A. Hallgarten

One cold winter day in the Swiss Alps, a lone traveler knocked on the door of a monastery and asked for shelter. As he was about to depart the following morning and after glancing at the dark, snowy sky, he asked the monk if the famous St. Bernard dogs, with the cask of brandy around their necks were still available for rescue work.

The monk replied that system was not used in these modern times, but that they had a new, far better method available. He then gave the traveler a small bottle of Vermouth and a small bottle of Gin and said, "Now if the snow is coming down and you get lost - just take out the bottle of Vermouth and the bottle of Gin and start to mix them - and in a matter of seconds four to five people will arrive and say *That's No Way To Make A Martini!*"

George & Sally Dietz
(US Foreign Service, Ret.)

After four martinis, my husband turns into a disgusting beast. And after the fifth, I pass out altogether.

Anon.

Livy my darling,
I want you to be sure
to have in the bathroom when I arrive,
a bottle of Scotch
whisky, a lemon, some
crushed sugar and a
bottle of Angostura
bitters. Ever since I
have been in London
I have taken in a wine
glass what is called a
cocktail (made with
these ingredients)
before breakfast, before
dinner and just before
going to bed ...
    To it I attribute the
fact that up to this day
my digestion has been
wonderful ...simply
perfect.
    Mark Twain
(in a letter to his wife)

The most common and wonderful
Guinness concoction is the Black
Velvet; that wondrous, almost sedative-
like drink of equal parts champagne
and Guinness that was the favorite
of the German statesman, Bismarck.
The Black Velvet was first served in
observance of the death of Queen
Victoria's husband, Prince Albert, in
1861. The champagne portion stood
for the nobility and the Guinness represented the common class who
adored Albert. The resulting blend
produced one of the world's best
cocktails.
    Alan D. Eames

The first Bloody Mary was mixed in
1924 at Harry's Bar in Paris by a bartender named Fernand Petiot. ... The
drink was probably named after Mary
Tudor, the Roman Catholic daughter
of Henry VIII, who was known as
Bloody Mary due to her penchant for
executing Protestant subjects in order
to save their souls.
    Carol Harralson

75

I had gone the evening before to La Floridita, Hemingway's favorite bar in Havana to do my 'homework' and sample his favorite concoction, the daiquiri. But no one can be overprepared! When, at nine the next morning, Hemingway called from the kitchen, 'What will you have to drink?' my reply was, I thought letter-perfect: 'Daiquiri, sir.' 'Good God, Karsh,' Hemingway remonstrated. 'at *this* hour of the day?'

Yousuf Karsh

(on preparing to photograph Ernest Hemingway)

"The Highball" : was named after a railroad signal that came into use in the last part of the 19th century. A ball was placed on top of a pole to signal to the engineer that all was clear and he could proceed at full throttle. The signal was called a 'highball' and the railroad workers started using the term as a name for a Whiskey and Water, or a Whiskey and Soda. Today a highball can be any tall drink containing liquor and a mixer.

Jon Buller

The Manhattan cocktail was invented in 1874 by Jenny Jerome (Winston Churchill's mother). She was throwing a party for Sam Tilden at the exclusive Manhattan Club, Madison Avenue at 26th Street. With the reluctant head-bartender, she concocted the opposite of the Martini by uniting some excellent whiskey with a lesser potion of herb-piqued wine (sweet vermouth), aromatic bitters and a Maraschino cherry. They named it after the Manhattan Club and it went into mixology history.

Mark Pollman

There was a young lady of Trent,
Who said that she knew what it meant
    When men asked her to dine
    With cocktails and wine,
She knew what it meant - but she went.

Anon.

Gimme a viskey, ginger ale on the side, and don't be stingy, baby.

Greta Garbo
as Anna Christie
(the first time she spoke on screen)

You can always tell that the crash is coming when I start getting tender about Our Dumb Friends, Three highballs and I think I'm St. Francis of Assisi.

Dorothy Parker

I was sitting before my third or fourth Jellybean - which is anisette, grain alcohol, a lit match, and a small, wet explosion in the brain.

Louise Erdrich

76

Some unknown admirer of his books and mine sent to the hotel a most enormous mint julep, wreathed in flowers. We sat, one on either side of it, with great solemnity (it filled a respectably-sized round table) but the solemnity was of very short duration. It was quite an enchanted julep, and carried us among innumerable people and places that we both knew. The julep held out far into the night, and my memory never saw him afterwards otherwise than as bending over it, with his straw, with an attempted air of gravity (after some anecdote involving some wonderfully droll and delicate observation of character), and then as his eye caught mine, melting into that captivating laugh of his, which was the brightest and best that I have ever heard.

Charles Dickens

(on drinking with Washington Irving in Baltimore, Md.)

In 1896 the Bacardi company's fortunes received another boost when an American mining engineer who wished to develop something special for some visiting friends, first hit upon the happy combination of light Bacardi rum and lime juice as a cocktail. The American was Jennings Cox who was working a series of copper mines in the Sierra Maestra mountains outside Santiago in Cuba near a hamlet called Daiquiri. The mines bore the name of that hamlet. When Cox's friends expressed their delight with his new drink, asking what it was, he chose to name it after the mines and called it the Daiquiri.

Bacardi Company information sheet

Nothing is out of date about the **Old Fashioned!**

Charlie Clarke

Beer & Brewers

Reasons For Drinking Beer:

Beer is sacred business, a mood-altering food substance that may have preserved the human species. To drink beer is to be human. *Alan D. Eames*

There is nothing for a case of nerves like **a case of beer.** *Joan Goldstein*

Beer is an improvement on water itself. *Grant Johnson*

Beer has long been the prime lubricant in our social intercourse and the sacred throat-annointing fluid that accompanies the ritual of mateship. To sink a few cold ones with the blokes is both an escape and a confirmation of belonging. *Rennie Ellis* (on drinking beer in Australia)

Just relax, stay inside and open a six-pack. *Buffalo mayor James Griffin* (on what to do during the heavy snow season)

This is no mere beverage, this glass of beer. It is a small miracle. It is the drink of worship in millions of grottos, forests, temples and secret grounds that have now receded into dark thousands of years before man's recorded history.

It is the laughter and fighting boasts of a million men from the Norseland. It is the chanting of a million monks of the church who reverently thought of bread and beer as one. It is the jollity of songs and toasts bellowed in a million taverns and flung to the stars in a thousand tongues across the centuries.

It is the grains of the earth growing in the ground under the blazing sun and the night mists of the plains girdling the planet, and of barley seed grown rich and golden.

And it is the men who turned to the craft of brewing - at first with awe and then with growing art and science and love - and made it into one of the great achievements of man's accommodation to his natural environment. *Frederic Birmingham*

Give me a woman who truly loves beer, and I will conquer the world. *Kaiser Wilhelm*

There is something in the composition and effect of malt liquors which supplies a want in the national characters and physiques of the most intellectual, vigorous, and progressive countries of the globe.

One Hundred Years Of Brewing

80

27 Reasons Why BEER Is Better Than A WOMAN!

1. You can enjoy Beer all month long.
2. Beer stains wash out.
3. You don't have to wine and dine a Beer.
4. Your Beer will always wait patiently for you in the car.
5. When a Beer goes flat, you toss it.
6. Beer is never late.
7. Hangovers go away.
8. A beer doesn't get jealous when you grab another Beer.
9. Beer never has a headache.
10. When you go to a bar, you can always pick up a Beer.
11. After a Beer, the bottle is still worth a nickel.
12. A Beer won't get upset when you come home with Beer on your breath.
13. If you pour a Beer right, you know you'll always get good head.
14. You can have more than one Beer a night and not feel guilty.
15. You can share a Beer with your friend.
16. A Beer always goes down easy.
17. You always know you're the first one to pop a Beer.
18. A Beer is always wet.
19. Beer doesn't demand equality.
20. You can have a Beer in public.
21. A Beer doesn't care when you come.
22. A frigid Beer is a good Beer.
23. You don't have to wash a Beer before it tastes good.
24. It's good to get a case of Beer.
25. It's acceptable to be in public with a dark Beer.
26. Aging is good for Beer.
27. Having a Beer with nuts is alright.

Anon.

WE DON'T SELL BEER, WE RENT IT!

Restroom Grafitti

A hygienic drink is a useful comestible, an excellent digestive and a helper of nutrition, which every man who considers his health must think of using.

Louis Pasteur

Each of us is a beer expert. We know what tastes good. Understanding beer deepens our pleasure, but it all comes down to that first **ah**.

Stephen Dinehart

He had his beer
From year to year
And then his bier had him.

Anon. (Pun obviously intended)

Beer commercials are so patriotic: "Made the American Way." What does that have to do with America? Is that what America stands for? Feeling sluggish and **urinating frequently**?

Scott Blakeman

How do you know? It could have been Schlitz.

Earl Campbell

(after a bottle of beer was thrown at him and a security guard said 'That was bush.')

EXPRESS LANE:

5

BEERS OR LESS!

Bar Sign over Men's urinal at *Ed Debevic's*, Chicago

Show me a nation whose national beverage is beer, and I'll show you an advanced toilet technology.

Mark Hawkins

82

Who Drinks Beer

Men will not do without beer. To prohibit it and secure total abstinence is beyond the power of the sages.

Shu Ching

There's 150 million times more beer drinkers than there is Presidents.

Billy Carter

Among Babe Ruth's pallbearers on that muggy day, August 16, 1948, were Joe Dugan and Waite Hoyt, Ruth's old Yankee teammates.

"I'd give a hundred bucks for an ice cold beer," Dugan whispered, sweating under the burden of the coffin. "So would the Babe," Hoyt whispered back.

Lawrence S. Ritter

To dive into the stands for a popup, catch the ball, and at the same time grab a guy's beer and take a big swig.

George Brett
(on his baseball fantasy)

Twenty, thirty beers before a game never hurt anybody. *Lucien Dechene*
(hockey goalie)

Beer is the mother's milk of American Legion picnics ... God, do not take from us our beer.

Senator Thomas Eagleton

The Quality Of Beer

You can't be a true bleacher creature drinking this kind of beer. *Stan Johnson*
(on low calorie beer sold at Tiger Stadium)

This could legally have been sold in the United States during Prohibition.

Critic tartly commenting on a characterless, mass-produced beer.

"Looks like rain."
"Aye, and it don't *taste* much like beer, either."

Two Yorkshiremen in their local pub.

83

An Englishman is asked by an American to explain the difference between British beers and American beers.

The Brit answers, "If you put a light-bodied American beer next to a heavy full-bodied British beer it's like making love in a canoe - Fuckin' near water!"

Mark Pollman

HOW TO DRINK BEER:

"Did you ever taste beer?"
"I had a sip of it once,"
said the small servant.
"Here's a state of things!"
cried Mr. Swivvler
"She NEVER tasted it -
it can't be tasted in a sip."

Charles Dickens

Kindly observe the tankard of beer I have offered to you. This beer was not simply made to drink. It was made to speak to you. And if you, with your tankard of beer, could learn the dialogue, you would discover that in your tankard lives a *Milky Way* of tiny bubbles. And inside each bubble, there exists an idea that is just waiting to be discovered. Each one of these ideas can make you grand and large and fortunate if you so desire to learn to talk to beer.

M. Bellot

Beer is a light, narcotic, alcoholic beverage, which charms us into a state of gladness and soft hilarity; it protects our hearts against stings of all kinds, awaiting us in this valley of misery; it diminishes the sensitiveness of our skin to the nettles and to all the bites of the numberless, detestable human insects that hum, hiss and hop about us. The happy mortal who has elected beer as his preferred stimulant imbeds greater griefs and joys in soft pillows; surely thus being wrapped up he will be able to travel through this stormy life with less danger.

Yes, I find such a perfection of forms, such as a softness and ductility of the tissue in the pale juice of barley, that I, to express its physiology with a few words, might say: "It is to us in our lifetime like a wrapper which enables our fragile nature unendangered to reach the safe port." *Paolo Montegazza MD*

PORTER

ALES &

But if at the Church they would give us some ale,
And a pleasant fire our souls to regale,
We'd sing and we'd pray all the livelong day,
Nor ever once wish from the Church to stray.

William Blake

Life isn't all beer and skittles; but beer and skittles,
or something of the same sort, must form a good
part of every Englishman's education.

Thomas Hughes

That a glass of bitter beer or pale ale, taken with
the principal meal of the day, does more good
and less harm than any medicine the physician
can prescribe.

Dr Carpenter

[Porter] ... a wholesome liquor which enables the
London porter-drinkers to undergo tasks that
ten gin-drinkers would sink under.

John Bickerdyke

Say for what were hopyards meant,
Or why was Burton built on Trent?
Oh many a peer of English brews
Livelier liquor than the Muse,
And malt does more than Milton can
To justify God's ways to man.
Ale, man, ale's the stuff to drink
For fellows whom it hurts to think:
Look into the pewter pot
To see the world's as the world's not.

A. E. Housman

He that buys land buys many stones;
He that buys flesh buys many bones;
He that buys eggs buys many shells;
He that buys good ale buys nothing else.

English proverb

85

STOUTS & GUINNESS

An Irishman is a simple machine for converting **Guinness** into urine.
Anon.

Ireland is still the country where a 'blonde in black' refers not only to a beautiful woman but to a pint of **Guinness.** *Sybil Taylor*

As we read in the first chapter of Guinness'es. *James Joyce*

Guinness brewery Ad slogan:
"Over nine million Guinnesses are drunk every day."
Popular retort:
"I didn't know it was such a large family."

THE HISTORY OF BEER

The drinking of beer is universal. It is older than history and more common than the conduct of business, or the creation of art. And we'll be there as long as there are friends to toast one another's health, as long as people need a way to say, "here's to the future."
John Rogers

My people drink beer. His majesty was brought up on beer and so were his ancestors and his officers and soldiers. Many battles have been fought and won by soldiers nourished on beer, and the King does not believe that coffee-drinking soldiers can be depended on to endure hardships or to beat the enemies.
Frederick the Great (King of Prussia)

What two ideas are more inseparable than beer and Britannia? - what event more awfully important to an English colony, than the erection of the first **brewhouse**?
Reverend Sydney Smith

The nation has arbitrarily stupefied itself for nearly a thousand years: nowhere have the two great European narcotics, alcohol and Christianity, been more wickedly misused ... How much moody heaviness, lameness, humidity, and dressing-gown mood, how much beer is in German intelligence!
Friedrich Nietzsche

86

A moderate use of beer will aid digestion, quicken the powers of life, and give elasticity to the body and mind.

1866 US Department of Agriculture report

I do not whine as others may
Of money I've misused;
Ah no, I only think today
Of pints that I've refused ...

Dryblower Murphy

Beer relaxes and creates contentment, drawing friends and neighbors together. ... Beer is the beverage of celebration, of the shared harvest and communal prosperity. It's what we drink at town festivals and picnics in the park, beach parties and block parties, family reunions and friendly get-togethers. From the Goddess of Beer to Spuds McKenzie, on Oktoberfest or the Fourth of July, at Sunday afternoon baseball or Alderman Riley's re-election, beer is the drink of parties and holidays, the ritual substance that unites us all.

Bruce Aidells and Denis Kelly

The Brewers & The Breweries

Imagine the outcry from the Black community if a brewer were to make a liquor entitled *Martin Luther King Beer* or from the Christian community for a *Jesus Christ White Wine.*

Gregg Bourlann
(Chairman, Cheyenne River Sioux tribe in South Dakota on Hornell Brewing naming its new Malt Liquor *Crazy Horse*)

Blessed is the mother who gives birth to a brewer.

old Czech saying

You don't make beer, you get everything together as best you can. Then you let the beer make itself.

Fritz Maytag

Charlemagne himself was the personal tutor and trainer of the brewers of his realm; he intended to have no inferior brew for the people who were to call him The Great.

Federic Birmingham

On his deathbed, while holding up a bottle of Budweiser, the last thing that Gussie Busch must have said to his son, August III was, **"Hey, kid, it ain't broken - don't try to fix it!"**

Mark Pollman
(on the fact that 25% of all beer sold in the US is Budweiser)

87

I have come to the conclusion that the Germans love beer ... The moment I crossed the frontier from wine-drinking France I smelt hops and I have smelt hops ever since ... go where you will, with the aroma from beer shops and breweries, and there is no denying the fact that the two great industries of the German nation are hop raising and beer drinking, the women attending to the former and the men to the latter.

In my innocence I once thought that beer drinking in England was carried to excess, but I was mistaken. Englishmen are the infant class - in the ABC's - in acquiring a German's education in the practice of beer drinking.

Henry Ruggles

You can only drink

30 or 40

glasses of beer a day, no matter how rich you are.
Adolphus Busch

I really like your beer.
Dave LaPointe
(after meeting then vice president Bush)

It is my aim to win the American people over to our side, to make them all lovers of beer and teach them to have respect for the brewing industry and the brewer. ... It may cost us a million dollars and even more, but what of it if thereby we elevate our position? I stand ready to sacrifice my annual profits for years to come if I can gain my point and make people look upon beer in the right light.

Adolphus Busch

Whisky & Whiskey

Reasons To Drink Whiskies:

I know folks all have a **tizzy** about it, but I like a little bourbon of an evening. It helps me sleep, I don't much care what they say about it.

Lillian Carter
(on attitudes toward drinking)

The Scottish genius for converting barley into the world's pre-eminent spirit - an art not a science, they say - has inspired poets, novelists, song-writers, journalists and the journey-men of the advertising world. Whisky has in it an infinite capacity to speed the pen to florid heights of hyperbole, much of which is no doubt deeply regretted the morning after.

Derek Cooper

"It's no the love o the drink that gars a body get the waur o't," remarked an old Scots worthy; *"it's the conveeviality o the thing."*

F. Marian McNeill

Leaning against the wind and rain, you drive off from the first tee at Machrie. You feel your ball has gone straight, so with head down you plod on ... Eighteen holes of that - and then a glass of Lagavulin! It's not that it revives you; it crawls along your fingertips and toenails in a divine glow ... But if I had been golfing in a hot sun at Eastbourne - would I have been looking forward to this potent stuff at the end?

(as told to Neil Gunn)

France has given claret to the world and the world is better for it. Scotland has it in its power to give to the world such whisky as few can dream of: and the world would again be better. Leoville, Margaux, and Latour might be matched with Islay, Glenfiddich and Glen Grant. Hout Brion, singing aloud, might hear in reply the *voix d'or* of Highland Park.

And the brown streams of Glenlivet would need not envy the sun-warmed slopes of Bordeaux.

With such whisky to help it the world would grow kindlier and more wise, aware of beauty and comforted with friends.

Erik Linklater

90

A gulp of whisky at bedtime -
it's not very scientific, but it helps.

Alexander Fleming
British microbiologist
(when asked about a cure for colds)

There are only two things in life
that should be strong -
the whiskey and the woman
who pulls the plow!

S. McAllen

What butter or whiskey'll not cure,
there's no cure for.

Irish proverb

The northern nations are more
addicted to the use of strong
liquors than the southern, in
order to supply by art the want
of that genial warmth of blood
which the sun produces.

James Boswell

Women will be as pleasing to
men as whiskey when they learn
to improve as much with age.

Anon.

The advantages of whiskey
over dogs are legion.
Whiskey does not need to be
periodically wormed, it
does not need to be fed,
it never requires a special
kennel, it has no toenails to
be clipped or coat to be strip-
ped. Whiskey sits quietly in
its special nook until you want
it. True, whiskey has a nasty
habit of running out, but then
so does a dog.

W. C. Fields

91

Whisky has made us what we are. It goes with our climate and with our nature. It rekindles old fires in us, our hatred of cant and privilege, our conviviality, our sense of nationhood, and, above all, our love of Scotland. It is our release from materialism, and I often think that without it we should have been so irritatingly efficient that a worse persecution than the Hebrews ever suffered would have been our inevitable fate.

Sir Robert Bruce Lockhart

If you can't make seventy, without cigars and whisky - it ain't worth going!

Mark Twain

WHAT HAPPENS WHEN WHISKIES ARE DRUNK

Whisky, no doubt, is a devil; but why so many worshippers?

Lord Cockburn

One sip of this will bathe the drooping spirits in delight beyond the bliss of dreams.

John Milton

A **torchlight** procession marching down your throat.

John O'Sullivan

There's only one thing about whisky - it always looks so sober in a glass.

Anon.

It smells like gangrene starting in a mildewed silo, it tastes like the wrath to come, and when you absorb a deep swig of it you have all the sensations of having swallowed a lighted kerosene lamp.

A sudden violent jolt of it has been known to stop the victim's watch, snap his suspenders and crack his glass eye right across.

Irvin Shrewsberry Cobb

Whiskey has been blamed for lots it didn't do. It's a bravemaker. All men know it. If you want to know a man, get him drunk and he'll tip his hand. If I like a man when I'm sober, I kin hardly keep from kissing him when I'm drunk. This goes both ways. If I don't like a man when I'm sober, I don't want him in the same town when I'm drunk.

Charles Russell

Licker talks mighty loud w'en it gits loose from de jug.

Joel Chandler Harris

92

As long ago as 1950, when I was teaching at Cornell University, I introduced American friends to Mortlach, available at Macy's in New York, and they took to it with enthusiasm. Perhaps the fact that it matured in plain oak and was virtually colorless was held to be in its favor. I remember that I was asked to give a talk at the University on Scotch whisky and in the course of my remarks I observed that one of the "best buys" in pot-still Highland malt whisky was the Mortlach Available at Macy's.

The next time I went to Macy's to restock for myself I was told that they were out of stock. When I expressed astonishment, the assistant said: "Some damn fool professor at Cornell has been telling all his students to buy it, and we've run out."

David Daiches

**Ever see a bear cat hug a lion? No, good God, no.
Well, whiskey make rabbit hug lion, Yes, God, yes.**

American Negro song

HOW TO DRINK WHISKIES

You might make that a double.
Neville Heath
(when offered a drink by the prison governor before being executed for a double murder)

Whisky, properly savoured and not grossly gulped, is essentially a pensive and philosophic liquor.
Ivor Brown

Too much of anything is bad, but too much whiskey is just enough.
Mark Twain

A whisky bottle's an awfu' inconvenient thing; its owr muckle foe ane, an' nae eneuch for twa!

Old Highland lament

As a friend, whisky has virtues unequaled by any other form of alcohol. As an enemy there is no Scot who does not know its dangers and almost no Scottish family without its whisky skeletons. They rattle in my own cupboard and I myself have been near enough to destruction to respect whisky, to fear it, and to continue to drink it.
Sir Robert Bruce Lockhart

Never delay kissing a pretty girl or opening a bottle of whiskey.
Ernest Hemingway

93

SCOTCH & IRISH WHISKY

Whisky has more lovers and fewer friends than anything on earth.

Anon.

Keep your head cool and
your feet warm,
And a glass of good whiskey
will do you no harm.
Anon.

Whisky-tasting, like wine-
tasting or tea-tasting, is
an art which takes years
of study before it can be
mastered. *Sir Robert
Bruce Lockhart*

According to the law of Scotland
(which is quite a different ass from
the law of England), you are not
allowed to make water in public or
whisky in private! *Jack House*

We got at night to Inverary, where we
found an excellent inn ... We supped
well; and after supper, Dr. Johnson
whom I had not seen taste any fermented liquor during all our travels,
called for a gill of whisky. 'Come, let
me know what it is that makes a
Scotchman happy!' He drank it all
but a drop which I begged leave to
pour into my glass, that I may say we
had drunk whisky together.
Jack House

FREEDOM AND WHISKY GANG THEGITHER!
Robert Burns

There are two things that a Highlander
likes naked and one of them is malt whisky.
old Scottish saying

Stick to Scotch if you want to be brave,
gin only makes you piss.
*Clark Gable
(cautioning David Niven going off to the
front in World War II)*

This is smart stuff. *John Keats*
(on tasting whisky for the first time)

Scotch whisky to a Scotchman is as
innocent as milk to the rest of the
human race. *Mark Twain*

94

This swift and fiery spirit ... belongs to the alchemist's den and to the long nights shot with cold, flickering beams; it is compact of Druid spells and Sabbaths (of the witches and the Calvinists); its graces are not shameless, Latin, and abundant, but have a sovereign austerity, whether the desert's or the north wind's; there are flavours in it, insinuating and remote, from mountain torrents and the scanty soil on moorland rocks and slanting, rare sun-shafts.

Augustus Muir

To listen to the silence of five thousand casks of whisky in the twilight of a warehouse while the barley seed is being scattered on the surrounding fields might make even a Poet Laureate dumb.

Neil Gunn

Give an Irishman lager for a month and he's a dead man. An Irishman is lined with copper, and the beer corrodes it. But whiskey polishes the copper and is the saving of him.

Mark Twain

Poteen is just murder. It's the end, and you can take it from me, for I have had a wide enough experience of it.

Brendan Behan

A minister in a rural parish ... when out walking a day or two after his return from the General Assembly in Edinburgh was accosted by one of his parishioners. "I've just been up to the station, sir, and I see there's a wooden box lying there addressed to you."

"Quite so, Tammas, quite so. Just a few books I was buying when I was in Edinburgh."

"Aye. Imphm. Ah well, sir, I wadna be owre lang. They're leakin'."

Anon.

A favourite Irish story concerns the police sergeant who led a raid on an illicit still. "You know why we are here don't you?" he said to the proprietor of the still. "Indeed I do", was the reply. "But I'm terribly sorry I can't oblige you. We are out of stock at the moment."

Michael Jackson

Yolland: "Poteen - poteen - poteen. Even if I did speak Irish I'd always be an outsider here, wouldn't I? I may learn the password but the language of the tribe will always elude me, won't it. The private core will always be ... hermetic, won't it?"

Brian Friel

Here is to the Irish, a whiskey with heart,
that's smooth as a Leprechaun's touch,
yet soft in its taste as a mother's embrace
and a gentleness saying as much.   *Anon.*

BOURBON & AMERICAN WHISKEY

Bourbon whiskey taken without ice by American
statesmen and patriots has quickened the political process.
Bernard De Voto

I have found a way to make so good a drink of Indian
corn as I protest I have divers times refused to drink
good strong English beer and chosen to drink that.
Captain George Thorpe
(*on whiskey at Jamestown, early 17th century*)

There is a lot of nourishment in an acre of corn.
William Faulkner

Makes a feller wish he had a throat a mile long
and a palate at every inch of it.   *Anon.*

Bourbon does for me what the piece of cake
did for Proust.
Walker Percy

Let me tell you, suh, there's only one likker
that's properly qualified to caress a gentleman's
palate in the way a gentleman's palate deserves to
be caressed; and that's red likker - the true and
uncontaminated fruitage of the perfect corn, and
that, suh, is Bourbon. ... Take it straight, or in a
toddy or julep, but never otherwise under any
circumstances. For Bourbon stands on its own
merits - the king, suh, and the queen and the
whole family of likkers.
Irvin Shrewsberry Cobb

Well, between Scotch and nothin',
I suppose I'd take Scotch.
It's the nearest thing
to good moonshine I can find.
William Faulkner

96

CHAPTER EIGHT

Spirits and Other Boozes

BRANDY AND COGNACS

On Wednesday, April 7, I dined with him at Sir Joshua Reynold's. I have not marked what company was there. Johnson harangued upon the qualities of different liquors; and spoke with great contempt of claret, as so weak, that "a man would be drowned by it before it made him drunk." He was persuaded to drink one glass of it, that he might judge, not from recollection, which might be dim, but from immediate sensation. He shook his head, and said: "Poor stuff! No Sir, claret is the liquor for boys; port for men; but he who aspires to be a hero (smiling) must drink brandy. In the first place, the flavour of brandy is most grateful to the palate; and then brandy will do soonest for a what drinking *can* do for him. There are, indeed, few who are able to drink brandy. That is a power rather to be wished for than attained. And yet (proceeded he), as in all pleasure hope is a considerable part, I know not but fruition comes too quick by brandy. Florence wine I think the worst; it is wine only to the eye; it is wine neither while you are drinking it, nor after you have drunk it; it neither pleases the taste, nor exhilarates the spirits."
I reminded him how heartily he and I used to drink wine together, when we were first acquainted; and how I used to have a headache after sitting up with him. He did not like to have this recalled, or, perhaps thinking that I boasted improperly, resolved to have a witty stroke at me; "Nay, Sir, it was not the *wine* that made your head ache, but the *sense* that I put into it."

James Boswell

Dr Johnson's absurdly crude view that claret is a wine for boys, with port allotted to men, was never shared in Scotland.

Ivor Brown

For two intimates, lovers or comrades, to spend a quiet evening with a magnum, drinking no aperitif before, nothing but a glass of cognac after - that is the ideal! ... The worst time is that dictated by convention, in a crowd, in the early afternoon, at a wedding reception.

Evelyn Waugh

Winston Churchill's habit of guzzling a quart or two a day of good cognac is what saved civilization from the Luftwaffe, Hegelian logic, Wagnerian love-deaths, and the potato pancakes.
Charles McCabe

All alcoholic drinks, rightly used, are food for the body and soul alike, but as a restorative of both there is nothing like brandy.
George Saintsbury

Mike Hammer drinks beer and not cognac because I can't spell cognac.
Mickey Spillane

Have ready a bottle of brandy, because I always feel like drinking that heroic drink when we talk ontological heroics together.
Herman Melville
(to Nathaniel Hawthorne)

There is enough Napoleon brandy in novels to float a battleship.
Horace Annesley A. Vachell

Armagnac is what some of us think that cognac becomes when it grows up.
Mark Pollman

Good Armagnac can be very good and much better than ordinary Cognac, but the best Armagnac cannot hope to approach, let alone rival, the best Cognac.
André L. Simon

Brandy is lead in the morning, silver at noon and gold in the night.
old German proverb

If wine tells truth,
- and so have said the wise.-
It makes me laugh to think how brandy lies!
Oliver Wendell Holmes, Sr

Brandy *n.*
A cordial composed of one part thunder-and-lightning, one part remorse, two parts bloody murder, one part death-hell-and-the-grave, two parts clarified Satan and four parts holy Moses!
Dose, a headful all the time.
Brandy is said, by Emerson, I think, to be the drink of heroes. I certainly should not advise others to tackle it.
Ambrose Bierce

The great thing about making cognac is that it teaches you above everything else to wait - man proposes, but time and God and the seasons have got to be on your side.
Jean Monnet

99

There is a much quoted anecdote about the bishop of Angoulême who was introducing himself to a group of ecclesiastics.

"Bishop of Engolisma in the Charente", he proclaimed.
As this seemed to convey nothing to his peers, he added: "That means that I am bishop of Cognac."
Immediately their eyes lit up:

"Cognac, Cognac! What a splendid bishopric."

Anon.

Three cups of coffee and a shot of Cognac every day, rain or shine.

Ella Esser
(age 104, on her formula for long life, Rhinkerode, Germany 1955)

Red wine for children, Champagne for men, and brandy for soldiers.

Otto Von Bismarck

Cognac may be brandy, but all brandy isn't cognac! ... Some [brandies] are drinkable, mostly as a mixer, others are best used for removing tar stains from Volkswagens or stripping paint from old wooden dressers ... Cognac, however, is that special smooth, fragrant brandy produced in south-western France in an area defined by law in 1909.

Mike Lawrence

Call things by their right names - Glass of brandy and water! That is the current but not the appropriate name: ask for a glass of liquid fire and distilled damnation.

Robert Hall

It is the highest and noblest product of the age. I have a theory it is compounded of cherub's wings, the glory of a tropical dawn, the red clouds of sunset, and the fragments of lost epics by dead masters.

Rudyard Kipling
(on Button Punch using Pisco brandy)

Pour your brandy through the air into a bathtub or other large receptacle, from the top of the stairs, for example. Then put the vile stuff into bottles, with a plum in each, and let it stand without a cork for a week or three. Now add a single drop of maraschino liqueur to each bottle and seal it. You'll have fine old brandy. Now you can give it a funny name and drink it out of big round glasses, rolling it around, warming it with your hands, and smelling it like a dog.

Hilaire Belloc

If ever I marry a wife,
I'll marry a landlord's daughter,
For then I may sit in the bar,
And drink cold brandy and water.

Charles Lamb

PORT & SHERRY

If worldwide Port sales increased by more than twenty-five percent, there wouldn't be enough Port to go around. *Tim Sandeman*

Port is all mankind bottled. There are as many characters of port as of people, as many colors as races of mankind, and a good port lives to be as old as a man.
Antonio da Silva

Never have a small glass of port, my lad. It just goes rambling around looking for damage to do. ***Have a large glass.*** It settles down and does you good.
Lord Goddard

An aged Burgandy runs with the beardless Port. I cherish the fancy that Port speaks sentences of wisdom. Burgandy sings the inspired Ode.
George Meridith

It must appear strange to those who have always considered Port as the only wine suited for 'John Bull' and his climate, to learn how it was forced into use, only a century and a half ago... Although exceedingly fine when originally of a good vintage and of sufficient age, it may justly be objected that owing to the large portion of Brandy added even to the best ... the wine is rendered so powerful, that none but Englishmen can drink it.
Thomas George Shaw

Oh, the night porter's port
Is not the same sort
As the port that is brought
  by the day porter!
For the night porter's port's
Not a port but a tort,
While the day porter's port's
  from Oporto.
George Morrison

If penicillin can cure those who are ill, Spanish sherry can bring the dead back to life.
Sir Alexander Fleming
(discoverer of penicillin)

101

Senatorial Port! We cannot say that of any other wine. Port is deep-sea deep; mark the difference. It is in its flavour deep; mark the difference. It is the classic tragedy, organic in conception.

Neither of Hermitage nor of Hock can you say that it is the blood of those long years, retaining the strength of youth with the wisdom of age ... Port speaks in sentences of wisdom, Burgundy sings the inspired Ode.

George Meridith

In England, sherry is the symbol of hospitality at home ... An invitation to 'come over for a glass of sherry' promises a relaxed combination of friends, comfortable shoes, an old sweater, an occasion that no one will be using as part of life's strategic game plan.

Gerald Asher

Port is the woman of forty: stronger, richer, sweeter even than Burgundy; much more body in it but less bouquet; it keeps excellently and ripens with age and can only be drunk freely by youth; in maturity, more than a sip of it is apt to be heavy, and if taken every day it is almost certain to give gout. But if you are vigorous and don't fear the consequences, the best wine in the world is crusted Port, half a century old; it is strong, with divine fragrance - heady, intoxicating - but constant use of it is not to be recommended; it affects the health of even its strongest and most passionate admirers and brings them to premature death.

Frank Harris

Spain is a grand country for drinking ... because the Spaniards do not approach the matter too reverentially ... you would never catch the French calling one of their finest clarets 'Uncle Bill', which is, after all, the rough equivalent to 'Tio Pepe'.

Quentin Crewe

When asked for his opinion of Madeira presented by an East India Company officer, an Asian chief said he "thought it a juice extracted from women's tongues and lion's hearts; for, after he drank a sufficient quantity of it, he could talk forever, and also fight like the devil."

Anon.

The unearned increment of my grandfather's Madeira.

James Russell Lowell
(to Judge Hoar, commiserating with him on his sufferings with the gout.)

102

"Good faith", said the knight. "This same young sober-blooded boy doth not love me; nor a man cannot make him laugh; but that's no marvel, he drinks no wine. There's none of these demure boys come to any proof; for thin drink doth so overcool their blood, and making many fish meals, that they fall into a kind of male green sickness; and when they marry, they get wenches; they are generally fools and cowards; which some of us should be too but for inflammation.

A good sherris-sack hath a twofold operation in it; it ascends me into the brains; dries me there all the foolish, and dull and crudy vapors which environ it, make it apprehensive, quick, inventive, full of nimble, fiery and delectable shape, which delivered o'er to the tongue which is the birth, becomes excellent wit.

The second property of your excellent sherris is the blood, which before cold and settled left the liver white and pale, which is the badge of pusillanimity and cowardice, but the sherris warms it and makes it course from the inwards to the parts extreme. It illuminates the face, which as a beacon, gives warning to all the rest of this kingdom, man, to arm, and then the vital commoners and inland petty spirits muster me all to their captain, the heart; who, great and puffed up with this retinue, doth any deed of courage, and this valor comes of sherris; so that skill in the weapon is nothing without sack, for that sets it a-work; and learning a mere hord of gold kept by a devil, till sack commences it and sets it in active use ... If I had a thousand sons, the first human principle I would teach them should be, to forswear thin potations and to addict themselves to sack."

William Shakespeare

'Falstaff' [The most quoted tribute to wine in literature]

103

RUM

A Martinique rum is the perfect antidote for a rainy day.
Ernest Hemingway

The first time I played the Masters I was so nervous I drank a bottle of rum before I teed off. I shot the happiest 83 of my life.
Chi Chi Rodriguez

Rum, Jamaica rum, 'Tis the one commodity that reconciles me to these barbarous places! *John Gay*

The population of Sydney in 1806 was divided into two classes. Those who sold rum and those who drank it.
George Mackanness

Lord Horatio Nelson's last request, after taking a bullet from a sniper in the Battle of Trafalgar, was to be buried on British soil. His body was sealed in a large cask of Rum. A drunken sailor was later found tapping into that cask. Hence the sometimes used term in Britain for a dollop of Rum as '*Nelson's Blood*'.
Mark Pollman

All I can conscientiously assert in of this spirit (Rum) is that it is scarcely as injurious as gin, whiskey or brandy unless it be taken in greater quantities. Rum is the bane of nine-tenths of the lower order of English, Irish and Scots who come to these islands. Other Europeans are in general less addicted to intemperance, yet are, on the whole, not so sober a set as Africans and Creoles.
El Joseph

GIN

No man is genuinely happy, married, who has to drink worse gin than he used to drink when he was single.
H. L. Mencken

When the clergyman's daughter
Drinks nothing but water
She's certain to finish on gin.
Rudyard Kipling

Gin was mother's milk to her.
George Bernard Shaw

You will find me drinking gin
In the lowest kind of inn,
Because I am a rigid vegetarian.
G. K. Chesterton

104

[In the middle of the 18th century] Gin struck the typically beer-drinking English populace like a thunderbolt. Its social destructiveness was comparable to the effect whiskey later had upon the North American Indian cultures.

Wolfgang Schivelbusch

The shortest way out of Manchester is notoriously a bottle of Gordon's gin.

William Bolitho

Yes, if you drink liquor, **you won't have worms**.

Hack Wilson
(after manager Joe McCarthy attempted to teach him an object lesson by dropping a worm in a glass of gin and asking if he had learned anything)

The correct drink with this dish is a straight shot of room-temperature gin. I had a Gilbey's 1975, which is superb.

Russell Baker

Don't tell my mother I'm living in sin,
  Don't let the old folks know;
Don't tell my twin that I breakfast on gin,
  He'd never survive the blow.

A. P. Herbert

VODKA

The relationship between a Russian and a bottle of vodka is almost mystical.

Richard Owen

I would rather live in Russia on black bread and vodka than in the United States at the best hotels; America knows nothing of food, love or art.

Isadora Duncan

Vodka is the aunt of wine.
Russian proverb

Russians are merrier drinking - without it they cannot live.

(Prince Vladimir of Kiev giving an account of Russia's conversion to Christianity and his rejecting the offer of an embassy of abstaining Muslims to convert to Islam.)

The Russian Chronicle

It's the easier way to make heroes. Vodka purges the brain and expands the strength.

Guy Sajer

Sometimes the Russians supplied vodka to their storm battalions, and the night before the attack we could hear them roaring like devils.

Major General F. W. von Mallenthin

105

It's made from fermented Russian wheat, corn, oats, barley, alfalfa, or jimsonweed, just which ever one of these they happen to have handy. Then they start adding the ingredients.

Potato peelings is one of 'em, then Russian boot tops. You just take the tops of as many Russian boots as you can get when the men are asleep, you harvest 'em just above the ankle.

The next ingredient (the Russians always deny this to me, but I have always believed it's true) is the whiskers. They say that they don't put 'em in vodka, that they are only used in that soup called borsch.

Finally it's fermented and the Russian vodka is ready to drink.

When you do your eyes begin expanding, and your ears begin flopping like a mule's. It's the only drink where you drink and try to grit your teeth at the same time. It give the most immediate result of any libation ever concocted, you don't have to wait for it to act. By the time it reaches the Adam's apple it has acted. A man stepping on a red-hot poker can show no more immediate animation. It's the only drink where you can hit the man that handed it to you before he can possibly get away.

It's a timesaver. It should easily appeal to Americans, there is nothing so dull in American life as that period when a drinker is at that annoying stage. He is a pest to everybody, but vodka eliminates that, you are never at the pest period.

Will Rogers

What is the surviving Martini like? ... I conclude that vodka Martinis outnumber gin Martinis by at least three to two and probably by five to one - not surprising when one considers that vodka outsold gin by thirteen million cases in 1977. At most twenty percent and probably as few as five percent of all Martinis are now served straight up. In other words, today's martini is vodka on the rocks.

Lowell Edmunds

Aperitifs, Liqueurs & Words

... of all things he had enjoyed and forgotten and that came back to him when he tasted that opaque, bitter, tongue-numbing, brain-warming, stomach-warming, idea-changing liquid alchemy.

Ernest Hemingway
(on Absinthe)

In the 1880s, one distiller advertised his product so forcefully that he carved a permanent niche in our language. 'E.G. Booze' put his name on his whiskey and circulated it so widely that his name is one of the most common synonyms for liquor.

Carl H. Giles

Apart from cheese and tulips, the main product of the country is *advocaat*, a drink made from lawyers.

Alan Cohen

People may say what they like about the decay of Christianity; the religious system that produced green Chartreuse can never really die.

Saki

If you drink it straight down, you can feel it going into each individual intestine.

Richard Burton
(on 180 proof Raicilla)

What makes the cider blow its cork
With such a merry din?
What makes those little bubbles rise
And dance like harlequin?
It is the fatal apple, boys,
The fruit of human sin.

Christopher Morley

He ordered a Dubonnet on the rocks. A waiter who had known him from the old days looked shocked as he took the order.

"Dubonnet on the rocks?" he (Toots Shor) asked incredulously. "That's like putting a Band-Aid on a leper."

Bob Considine

Whenever whisky runs short the Yukoner falls back upon a villainous decoction known as 'hoochinoo' or 'hootch'.

Anon.

107

Among the Indians of the extreme north ... there is a liquor made which ... is called hoochinoo. The ingredients ... are simple and innocent, being only yeast, flour, and either sugar or molasses. *Edward R. Emerson*
(Hence, hooch.)

Marnier Lapostolle, a wealthy owner of vineyards, had once brought to Ritz a liqueur he had invented. Ritz tasted it and approved. Lapostolle decided to put it on the market, but he needed a name for it. Lapostolle was a little man, inclined to pomposity.
  Ritz said, half ironically, "Why not call it Le Grand Marnier?" Lapostolle did, and made a fortune.
Stephen Watts

If you've got schnapps, you're saved.
Wolfgang Borchert

I remember my introduction to Australian mead. It was a stinkingly hot day in late summer and, during a visit to McLaren, Vale (South Australia), we called at Daringa Cellars, which were without air conditioning. Ken Maxwell, the winemaker, insisted we sample his meads 'as they should be drunk' - in winter! While we were fanning ourselves, he disappeared ... Some minutes later he returned with his version of mulled mead ... As we discovered some months later, it is a divine refreshment to welcome anyone in from a bitter winter's night. *John Godde*

The great property of saké ... is that it provides the curious, almost sensual satisfaction that is derived from the warmth of the drink against the palate.
George Plimpton

Most of the people of Cathay drink wine of the kind that I shall now describe ... It is a liquor which they brew of rice, with a quantity of excellent spice in such a fashion that it makes a better drink than any other kind of wine; it is not only good but clear and pleasing to the eye, and being very hot stuff it makes one drunk sooner than any other wine. *Marco Polo*

Sake is the beautiful gift of Heaven. Drunk in small quantities it expands the heart, lifts the downcast spirit, drowns cares, and improves the health ... Enjoy sake by drinking just enough ... and thus enjoy seeing flowers when they are just bursting into bloom.
Kaibara Ekken

108

The Bubbly Stuff

Reasons For Drinking Champagne

Confucius once said that plain rice to eat, water to drink, and one's arm as a pillow were quite enough for earthly happiness.

Confucius was a wise and gentle soul ... but he never tasted champagne.

Ernst Hornickel

Chaque fois qu'un bouchon de champagne saute, une femme se met rir.
Every pop of a champagne cork sets a woman to laughing.

French proverb

Knock, Knock!
Who's there?
Fornication!
Fornication who?
For an occasion like this we really should have champagne.

Gene Karst

Of all the world's gastronomic delights, drinking champagne (... and the champagne ceremony) is probably the most satisfying sensual experience.

Issac Cronin & Rafael Pallais

Champagne, if you are seeking the truth, is better than a lie detector. It encourages a man to be expansive, even reckless, while lie detectors are only a challenge to tell lies successfully.

Graham Greene

Champagne: the great civilizer. *Talleyrand*

I like to start off my day with a glass of champagne. I like to wind it up with champagne, too. To be frank, I also like a glass or two in between. It may not be the universal medicine for every disease, as my friends the champagne people in Reims and Epernay so often tell me, but it does less harm than any other liquid.

Fernand Point

Do I like champagne? Ah, no, listen, that is a very personal question and one that I am not at liberty to answer ... A less intimate question, yes. You should have asked me when I last made love, for example. You should have asked me when I last made love and enjoyed it.

Henri Cartier-Bresson
(in response to a telephone survey)

110

The advantage of champagne consists not only in the exhilarating sparkle and play of its mantling life, where the beads that airily rise ever in the pursuit of those that have merrily passed; but in the magnetism it possesses above all other wines - of tempting the fair sex to drink an extra glass.
St. Ange

You know my way with the women; champagne's the thing; make 'em drink, make 'em talk; - make 'em talk, make 'em do anything.
William Makepiece Thackeray

Three be the things I shall ne'er attain: Envy, content, and sufficient champagne.
Dorothy Parker

If the aunt of the Vicar
Has never touched liquor
Look out when she finds the champagne.
Rudyard Kipling

WHAT HAPPENS WHEN DRINKING CHAMPAGNE

The sound of thy explosive cork, Champagne, has, by some strange witchery, of a sudden taught men the sweet music of speech. A murmur as of a rising storm runs round the table: badinage commences, flirtations flourish ... We might tell of breakfasts, and of suppers, suddenly converted from Saharas of intolerable dullness into oasises of smiles and laughter by the appearance of Champagne.
Charles Tovey

A single glass of champagne imparts a feeling of exhilaration. The nerves are braced; the imagination is stirred, the wits become more nimble.
Winston Churchill

Champagne's funny stuff. I'm used to whiskey. Whiskey is a slap on the back, and champagne's a heavy mist before my eyes.
James Stewart
(in the movie 'The Philadelphia Story')

That winter two things happened which made me see that the world, the flesh, and the devil were going to be more powerful influences in my life after all than the chapel bell. First, I tasted champagne; second, the theatre.
Belle Livingstone

111

Champagne has the taste of an apple peeled with a steel knife.
Aldous Huxley

Can you imagine opening a bottle of champagne with a bottle opener. I can't. It would eliminate half the fun.
Alain De Vogue

It has been said that the final sound from the uncorking of a bottle of Champagne is like the sigh of a contented woman.
Douglas Lamb

...champagne is the most exhilarating change from Bordeaux; it is like the woman of the streets; everybody that can afford it tries it sooner or later, but it has no real attraction. It must be taken in moderation: too much of it is apt to give a bad headache, or worse. Like a woman of the street, it is always within reach and its price is out of proportion to its worth.
Frank Harris

Champagne is the only wine to leave a woman beautiful after drinking.
Madame de Pompadour

WHO DRINKS CHAMPAGNE?

The way I gained my title's
By a hobby which I've got
Of never letting others pay
However long the shot;
Whoever drinks at my expense
are treated all the same,
From Dukes and Lords to
     cabmen down,
I make them drink Champagne.
Anonymous Music Hall Song

I'm only a beer teetotaler,
  not a champagne teetotaler.
George Bernard Shaw

There is no one so radical as a man-servant whose freedom of the champagne bin has been interfered with.
Tom Stoppard

Before I was born my mother was in great agony of spirit and in a tragic situation. She could take no food except iced oysters and champagne. If people ask me when I began to dance, I reply 'In my mother's womb, probably as a result of the oysters and champagne - the food of Aphrodite.'
Isadora Duncan

A top Hitler aide, on the role of champagne as a military thermometer:
On Hitler's 55th birthday, April 20, 1945, champagne wasn't served. It was only that day that I knew we had lost the war.
Issac Cronin & Rafael Pallais

Patriotism stops at champagne.
Otto Von Bismarck

How is champagne made?
By sheer genius, sir, sheer genius!
(Conversation at White's Club, London)

CHAPTER TEN

Wines & Bacchus

Reasons For Drinking Wine

If
God forbade drinking
would he have made
wine so good?
Cardinal Richelieu

If Heaven did not love wine,
Then there would be no wine star in Heaven.
If Earth did not love wine
There would be no wine springs on earth -
Why then be ashamed before Heaven to love wine?
Three cups, and one can perfectly understand the Great Tao;
A gallon, and one is in accord with all nature. *Li T'ai Po*

A cask of wine
works more miracles
than a church full of saints.
Italian proverb

What better adapted than the festive
use of wine in the first place to test and
in the second place to train the character
of a man, if care be taken in the use of it?
Where is there cheaper or more innocent?
Plato

Fermentation
is correlative
with life.

Wine is the
most healthful
and most
hygienic
of beverages.

Louis Pasteur

Clearly, the pleasures wines afford are transitory - but so are those of the ballet, or of a musical performance. Wine is inspiring and adds greatly to the joy of living.

Napoleon

Wine makes
daily living easier,
less hurried,
with fewer tensions
and more tolerance.

Benjamin Franklin

"In vino veritas," said the sage ... Before Noah, men having only water to drink, could not find the truth. Accordingly ... they became abominably wicked, and they were justly exterminated by the water they loved to drink. This good man, Noah, having seen that all his contemporaries had perished by this unpleasant drink, took a dislike to it; and God, to relieve his dryness, created the vine and revealed to him the art of making 'le vin'.

By the aid of this liquid he revealed more and more truth.

Benjamin Franklin

So wine-drinking should be encouraged in the same way that we try all the time to induce people to be more civilized, to have better meals, to live a more decent life, to appreciate better things altogether - it should be encouraged because it is pleasant and it is healthy.

X. M. Boulestin

(Wine) unlocks secrets, bids hopes be certainties, thrusts cowards into the fray, takes loads off anxious hearts, teaches new accomplishments. The life-giving wine cup ... whom has it not made free even in the pinch of poverty!

Horace

Name me any liquid - except our own blood - that flows more intimately and incessantly through the labyrinth of symbols we have conceived to make our status as human beings, from the rudest peasant festival to the mystery of the Eucharist. To take wine into our mouths is to savor a droplet of the river of human history.

Clifton Fadiman

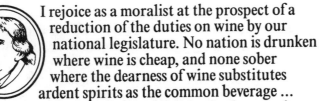

I rejoice as a moralist at the prospect of a reduction of the duties on wine by our national legislature. No nation is drunken where wine is cheap, and none sober where the dearness of wine substitutes ardent spirits as the common beverage ... Fix but the duty ... and we can drink wine here as cheap as we do grog and who will not prefer it? Its extended use will carry health and comfort to a much enlarged circle.

Thomas Jefferson

I am certain that the good Lord never intended grapes to be made into **grape jelly!**

Fiorello La Guardia

Who prates of war or want after taking wine?

Horace

When men drink, then they are rich and successful and win lawsuits and are happy and help their friends. Quickly, bring me a beaker of wine so that I may wet my mind and say something clever.   *Aristophanes*

Wine is earth's answer to the sun.

Margaret Fuller

Some drink, some drink here!
Bring those chestnuts from the wood of Estrocz;
With good new wine, you'll be composing some
fine farts.   *Rabelais*

We went to see the hermit in the mountain
He is plain and joyful
He lives on a handful of rice
The water in the spring contents him
And yet he has kept his wine cup.   *Li T'ai Po*

No thing more excellent nor more valuable than wine was ever granted mankind by God.

Plato

116

They went down in the cellar with Grampa and while he decapitated the flowers they looked at all the summer shelved and glimmering there in the motionless streams, the bottles of dandelion wine. Numbered from one to ninety-odd, there the ketchup bottles, most of them full now, stood burning in the cellar twilight, one for every living summer day.

"Boy," said Tom, "what a swell way to save June, July and August. Real practical."

Grandfather looked up, considered this, and smiled.

"Better than putting things in the attic you never use again. This way, you get to live the summer over for a minute or two here or there along the way through the winter, and when the bottles are empty the summer's gone for good and no regrets and no sentimental trash lying about for you to stumble over for forty years from now. Clean, smokeless, efficient, that's **dandelion wine**."

Ray Bradbury

WINE & HEALTH

Wine is at the head of all medicines ... Where wine is lacking drugs are necessary.

Babylonian Talmud

Wine is an appropriate article for mankind, both for the healthy body and for the ailing man.

Hippocrates

Penicillin cures, but wine makes people happy.

Sir Alexander Fleming

Wine, Women & Song

What man can pretend to be a believer in love who is an abjurer of wine?

Richard Brinsley Sheridan

Candy is dandy - but Liquor is quicker - but to Wine her is finer.

Ogden Nash

A loaf of bread, a jug of wine, and $65 thou.

Alan Koehler

Beaujolais Nouveau, unlike Women - is only really good when it's young.

Mark Pollman

Where there is no wine there is no love.

Euripedes

117

Red bordeaux is like the lawful wife: an excellent beverage that goes with every dish and enables one to enjoy one's food. But now and then a man wants a change, and champagne is the most complete and exhilarating change ... it is like a woman of the streets: everyone that can afford it tries it sooner or later, but it has no real attraction. Moselle is like the girl of fourteen to eighteen: quick on the tongue, with an exquisite, evanescent perfume, but little body. It may be used constantly and in quantities, but it must be taken young.

Frank Harris

Who Drinks Wine

Anyone who knows his history ... must surely know his wines.

Arnold Toynbee

There are people who have been known to prefer bad wine to good, just as there are men who are fascinated by bad women.

André L. Simon

To drink wine is to be a good Catholic ... To drink only water, and to have a hatred for wine, is pure heresy close to atheism.

Beroalde DeVerville

El vino es la teta de los viejos!
Wine is the tit of old people!

Spanish proverb

You appear to have emptied your wine-cellar into your book-seller.

Theodore Hook
(to a friend who made his publisher drunk at dinner)

WHAT HAPPENS WHEN WINE IS DRUNK

Wine is like sex in that few men will admit not knowing all about it.

Hugh Johnson

Wine brings to light the hidden secrets of the soul, gives being to our hopes, bids the coward flight, drives dull care away, and teaches new means for the accomplishment of our wishes. *Horace*

Some people spend the day in complaining of a headache, and the night in drinking the wine that gives it.

Johann Wolfgang von Goethe

I can truthfully say that since I reached the age of discretion I have consistently drunk more than most people would say was good for me. Nor do I regret it ... Often wine has shown me matters in their true perspective, and has, as though by the touch of a magic wand, reduced great disasters to small inconveniences.

Wine has lit up for me the pages of literature, and revealed in life romance lurking in the commonplace.

Wine has made me bold but not foolish; has induced me to say silly things but not to do them.

Under its influence words have often come too easily which had better not have been spoken, and letters have been written which had better not have been sent.

But if such small indiscretions standing in the debit column of wine's account were added up, they would amount to nothing in comparison with the vast accumulation on the credit side.

Alfred Duff Cooper

He talked with more claret than clarity. *Susan Ertz*

All wines are by their very nature full of reminiscence, the golden tears and **red blood of summers** that are gone.

Richard Le Gallienne

No longer drink water (exclusively), but use a little wine for thy stomach's sake and thine often infirmities.

Paul to Timothy 1, 5:23

Wine exalts the fantasy, makes the memory lucid, increases happiness, alleviates pain, destroys melancholy. It reconciles dreams, comforts old age, aids convalescence and gives that sense of euphoria by which life is made to run smoothly, tranquilly and lightly.

Jack D. L. Holmes

It is not for kings, O Lemuel, it is not for kings to drink wine; nor for princes strong drink: Lest they drink and forget the law, and pervert the judgment of any of the afflicted. Give strong drink unto him that is ready to perish, and wine unto those that be of heavy hearts. Let him drink, and forget his poverty, and remember his misery no more.

Proverbs 31:4

Wine was born, not invented ... like an old friend, it continues to surprise us in new and unexpected ways.

Dr Salvatore P. Lucia

119

Wine digesteth food and disperseth care and dispelleth flatulence and clarifieth the blood and cleareth the complexion and quickeneth the body and hearteneth the hen-hearted and fortifieth the sexual power in many, but to name its virtue would be tedious. In short, had not Allah forbidden it, there were nought on the face of the earth to stand in it stead.

ancient Mohammedan poet

What priest can join two lovers' hands,
But wine must seal the marriage-bands?
As is celestial wine was thought
Essential to the sacred knot,
And that each bridegroom and his bride
Believ'd they were not firmly ty'd
Till Bacchus with his bleeding tun,
Had finished what the priest begun.

The Compleat Vintner 1720

Because of our great wines. *Michel Lourie* French track coach
(on why France doesn't produce great athletes the way it produces great wine)

HOW TO DRINK WINE

You cannot know wine by the barrel.
George Herbert

Wine pours into our mouths, you can smell it, feel it and drink it. I prefer it to music, flowers or the heavens.
French Folk Song

Wine is made to be drunk as women are to be loved: profit by the freshness of youth or the splendor of maturity; do not await decrepitude.
Theophile Malvezin

The wine is the master's, the goodness is the butler's. *English proverb*

The man who likes wine is never a drunkard: his pleasure is not the senseless consumption of quantity, but the intelligent anticipation and appreciation of quality.
X. M. Boulestin

One last word: Never let a drunkard choose your wine. You may be sure he knows nothing about it. It is only sober people who know how to drink.
M. Constantin-Weyer

120

THE QUALITIES OF WINE

Tell people to trust their own palates, Tell people not to be intimidated by the gurus, snobs and yes, even the wine producer.
Tell people if they enjoy a wine, drink it and don't be concerned about whether or not they can articulate why they like it.
Wine is like music - you may not know what is good, but you know what you like!

Justin Meyer

Have you noticed how bread tastes when you have been hungry for a long time! ..Jesus Christ, how good it was!
   As for the wine, I sucked it all down in one draught, and it seemed to go straight into my veins and flow round my body like new blood.

George Orwell

Beer is made by men, wine by God!

Martin Luther

The important thing with the 1874 Lafite is to taste the wine in its historical context. In 1874 the Impressionists were painting, Brahams composing and Paris was just over the Commune.

Michael Broadbent

The whole attraction of wine is that no two bottles are exactly alike, so you have to keep your discrimination ever likely. The standardized article, however good, lulls to sleep this very touchstone of a civilized man.

Edward Bunyard

The wines that one remembers best are not necessarily the finest that one has tasted, and the highest quality may fail to delight so much as some far more humble beverage drunk in more favorable circumstances.

H. Warner Allen

"I rather like bad wine", said Mr Mountchesney, "one gets so bored with good wine".

Benjamin Disraeli

The best use of bad wine is to drive away poor relations.

French proverb

What is the definition of a good wine? It should start and end with a smile.

William Sokolin

121

A bunch of grapes is beautiful, static and innocent; it is merely fruit. But when it is crushed it becomes an animal, for the crushed grapes become wine and wine has an animal life.

Wine suffers a heaving birth. It has a rough, groping childhood. It develops into adolescence. Then, if it does not sicken, it matures; and in this it is almost human since it does not mature according to the law of its particular and individual personality.

William Younger

What is man, when you come to think upon him, but a minutely set, ingenious machine for turning with infinite artfulness, the red wine of Shiraz into **urine**?

Isak Dinesen

The soft extractive note of an aged cork being withdrawn has the true sound of a man opening his heart.

William Samuel Benwell

Don't you hate people who drink white wine? I mean, my dear, every alcoholic in town is getting falling-down drunk on white wine. They think they aren't drunks because they only drink wine. Never, never trust anyone who asks for white wine. It means they're phonies.

Bette Davis

WINES OF COUNTRIES

The wines they drink in Paradise
They make in Haute Lorraine.

G. K. Chesterton

Burgundy tastes of cooked grapes.

Bordelais proverb

The best wines grow just about the château, but though this estate [Hochheim] gives its name to all the white wine of the neighborhood very little, if any, of the real Hock reaches England. Indeed I am told it is a wine used almost as a medicine. The Johannisberg wine is the real 'nectar of the Rhine', as the Germans term it … The hill on which it is raised is sheltered by the bend of the Rhine and by the range of the Tannus Mountains from all the harsh winds, and the sun shines on it all day long. This lovely region of the Rheingau is spoken of with ecstasy by the Germans and one of their writers calls it 'a piece of heaven that has fallen to earth'.

Washington Irving

122

The new curé ... set about recruiting and converting. But he realized he would have no influence over the men unless he could be rated a good connoisseur of wine, wine being the only concern at Clochemerle. Intelligence was measured by the finesse of the palate. Whoever, on three gulps swished round the gums, could not say: "Brouilly, Fleurie, Morgan or Juliénas", was considered a prize idiot by those fervent wine growers ...

Inspired with evangelical conviction, he began to frequent the inn and to take a glass of wine with one and the other of Torbayon's customers ...

The system did not bring a single soul back to God. But Ponosse acquired real proficiency in the matter of wines, and thereby gained the respect of the vine growers of Clochemerle ... In fifteen years Ponosse's nose flowered magnificently, becoming a huge Beaujolais nose, the shade of which was somewhere between canon's purple and cardinal-ate crimson. His nose inspired confidence in the region.

Gabriel Chevallier

If you wanted to open a sausage shop - hang giant liver-wursts and salamis right in the window - a terrific name for the shop would be Gewüurztraminer ... Which wine snob, I ask you, will order Schloss Vollrads - a sound likened to a tire going flat - when he could have an Amarone and a thousand violins?

Leonard S. Bernstein

There is a picture in mind of being on a very high-falutin' wine tour in Italy and looking out of the place from where the experts were tasting, across some farmland opposite; and there, an Italian laborer at his midday meal time picking the shelter of about the only tree within a half a mile. Under the boughs he sat down with a great sausage sandwich and a bottle of wine.

What a fool to wonder what the label was. Of course, there was no label. That was his wine, he made it - or his brother, or his uncle, father or grandfather: They drank wine automatically.

John Arlott

The smack of California earth shall linger on the palate of your grandson.

Robert Louis Stevenson

123

When I am asked, as I sometimes am, what is the bottle of wine I have most enjoyed, I have to answer that it was probably some **anonymous Italian fiasco** that I drank one starlit Tyrrhenian night under a vine-covered arbor, while a Neapolitan fiddler played 'Come Back To Sorrento' over the veal cutlet of the young woman I had designs on …

For not only is taste in wine as subjective as taste in women, but its enjoyment depends more on circumstances than does that of almost any other pleasure.

Cyril Ray

A Bordeaux wine merchant called on me the other day, and, in order to improve the occasion, I had up a bottle of Auldana, and asked him what it was. He said that I must pardon him for his want of familiarity with Burgundy, but he supposed it to be Pomard, and greatly he stared when I told him it was Australian, for no Frenchman can conceive of any wine that is not French.

Dr Robert Druitt

Wine Talk, Tastings & Snobs:

In Europe then we thought of wines as something as healthy and normal a food and also as a great giver of happiness and well being and delight. Drinking wine was not a snobbism nor a sign of sophistication nor a cult; it was as natural as eating and to me as necessary.

Ernest Hemingway

There is more rubbish talked about wine and wine tasting than anything else. It is the perfect subject for the snob, the bore … and they become more banal as time goes on.

Andre Launay

A wine label is like a person's face. It should tell you what you want to know about him.

Walter S. Taylor

Okay, so it has sophisticated assertiveness, presumptuous breeding, crisp authority, complex balance, elegant power, and respected finesse: *What's it taste like?*

Anon.

My belief is, that if a sample of wine were given to an analyst, marked 'poison' so that he would neither smell nor taste it, he could by no test yet known in chemistry affirm that it was wine at all.

Don Pedro Verdad

When it came to writing about wine, I did what almost everybody does - **faked it**.

Art Buchwald

A peculiar subgenre of the English language ... has flowered wildly in recent years, like some pulpy jungle plant. It's called Winespeak.
Frank J. Prial

I was convinced forty years ago - and the conviction remains to this day - that in wine tasting and wine talk there is an enormous amount of humbug. *T. G. Shaw*

The aristocrat of the table, the nature's gentleman of the cellar, the true amateur, the deeply knowledgeable, is rarely, if ever, a snob. *Michael Broadbent*

What Freud was to psychoanalysis, I was to wine.
Sam Aaron, owner
(Sherry-Lehmann Wines and Spirits)

A young man, invited to a winemen's dinner, invited to give his opinion on one of the wines, held his glass to the light, put it under his nose, surveyed the ceiling with puckered forehead, tasted a little, rolled it once round his mouth, chewed it, consented to swallow, sniffed once more, and finally observed, "Well, I should call it quite a friendly little wine but - er - scarcely intimate."

Upon which a hard-baked member of the Viticulture Society, sitting alongside asked him, "Did you really expect it to stand up and embrace you?" Only the word he used was not 'embrace' but something shorter and less delicate! *Walter James*

125

A bunch of us black-belt wine snobs were sitting around at dinner discussing some of the urgent social matters of the hour, like whether or not the '61 Latour was ready to drink ...

The waiter arrived, and Reginald, our guiding spirit, ordered a Châteauneuf-du-Pape with mignonettes of lamb bordelaise. We turned to him aghast.

"Surely, Reginald, a red Bordeaux would be more compatible," someone said.

"Possibly a Clos de Vougeot, or any good red Burgundy would be more subtle."

"Perhaps even a Rhine," I said, straining to appear both daring and sophisticated. "Why are you ordering a Châteauneuf-du-Pape?"

"Because I like the way it sounds," said Reginald.

Indeed, it has been said of Châteauneuf-du-Pape that more bottles have been ordered because of the name than because of the wine ... Wine snobs fear to admit it, but privately concede that they prefer the sound of a snappy Pouilly-Fuissé to a cumbersome and plodding Muscadet...

Pouilly-Fuissé ... a charming, flutelike sound, like the flight of a hummingbird or a quickly stolen kiss ... Amarone ... a wine of incredible depth, bouquet and breed. Forget about that, however, and listen to the name - preferably pronounced by Luciano Pavarotti - Am-Mahr-roh-nay; a siren song, a seduction.

Leonard S. Bernstein

A sight of the label is worth fifty years experience.

Michael Broadbent

The wine snob is a product of enthusiasm. His interest in labels, châteaux and years ... is apt, however, to rob him of pleasure ... He frequently deprives himself - as no Frenchman, however wealthy in bottles and knowledge of wine, does - of the simple pleasure of humbly nameless but eminently drinkable French table wines.

John Arlott

An old wine-bibber having been smashed in a railway collision, some wine was poured on his lips, to revive him.
"Paulillac, 1873", he murmured and died.

Ambrose Bierce

Watch out when the auctioneer calls some 19th century wine *"a graceful old lady whose wrinkles are starting to show through layers of make-up."* That means the wine is undrinkable, and some fool will spend $500 for it.

Robert Parker

Every important wine region in Europe is situated near a river. You need a lot of water to make a good wine.

Emile Peynaud
(Oenology Professor, University of Bordeaux)

You say man learned first to build a fire and then to ferment his liquor. Had he but reversed the process we should have no need of flint and tinder to this day.

Anon.

Some contend it started the first stable community life. Early man was nomadic. Several years are required to develop a producing vineyard, however, and the anthropologists say that pursuit of wine marks the change from a scattered human race to a settled one. It may well be that man was brewer before baker; lover of liquor before lover of home.

Morris E. Chafetz

Girls and vineyards are hard to guard.
Portugese proverb

But November 11 in France is not only St. Martins Day - the patron saint of reformed drunkards - but the feast of Bacchus, and the event was celebrated centuries back by joyful tasting of the new wine, or as Rabelais called it *"September Purée"*.

It would come as no surprise to read in Pantagruel, *"Busvons, car Beausjolai Nousveau est arrivé."*

Jennifer Taylor

On my way to this town [Beaune] I passed the stretch of the Côte d'Or, which, covered with a mellow autumn haze, with the sunshine shimmering through, looked indeed like a golden slope. One regards with a kind of awe the region in which the famous crûs of Burgundy (Vougeot, Chambertin, Nuits, Beaune) are, I was going to say, manufactured.

Adieu paniers; vendanges sont faites!

The vintage was over; the shrunken russet fibres alone clung to their stick. The horizon on the left on the road had a charm, however; there is something picturesque in the big, comfortable shoulders of the Côte.

Henry James

127

Buying a winery here is like buying a piece of fine art. It's like purchasing a Rembrandt or Picasso.

Bob Dwyer
(Napa Valley Growers' Association)

About mid-Winter every year I remember the inevitable smart guy. The one who, having looked us over very carefully during a typical Summer afternoon says, "Now what happens in Winter? I suppose you lock the door and go to the Caribbean!"

Well, I wish he could see us now, knee deep in snow (or mud) and very busy. Pruning has been underway with the crew braving the elements since Thanksgiving and the work is only 50% complete. With 25,000 vines to prune and each plant requiring about 10 - 15 minutes, this translates to over 4,000 man hours over four months shared by five people. For many weeks the workers are in colorful foul weather gear plus long johns. Meanwhile, the winery is undergoing major surgery, etc., etc.

Lolly Mitchell
(Sakonnet Vineyards, Rhode Island)

The discovery of a wine is of greater moment than the discovery of a constellation. The universe is too full of stars.

Brillat-Savarin

128

CHAPTER ELEVEN

Toasts For Special Occasions

George Bernard Shaw, attending a party, and called upon to deliver an after-dinner toast on the subject of sex, which at the turn of the century was considered an audacious word.

Shaw stood, raised his glass, addressed the guests by saying: **"It gives me great pleasure ..."** and sat down.

The frequency of drinking the King's health had actually threatened to disturb the peace of the realm.

F. W. Hackwood

We never *eat* anybody's health, always *drink* it. Why should we not stand up now and then and eat a tart to somebody's success?

Jerome K. Jerome

Drink to all healths,
but drink not to thine own.

Bishop Joseph Hall 1597

A toast:

Here's to **John** and ~~Mary~~;
May you never Lie,
May you never Cheat,
May you never Drink.
But if you must Lie -
Lie in each others' arms,
And if you must Cheat -
Cheat death,
And if you must Drink -
Drink with us because we love you!

Irish weddings
(as done by Dennis G. Hennessy)

a toast Answer:
Drink to me. Who am I to question genius?

(Pablo Picasso's last words)

A toast:
Drink to fair woman,
who, I think,
Is entitled to it;
For if ever anything
could drive me to drink,
She certainly could do it.

A toast:
Give Champagne and
fill it to the brim,
I'll toast in bumpers
every lovely limb!

Lord Chesterfield

130

A toast:

Here's to Woman, like a clinging vine
That blooms once a month and bears every nine.
She's the only living creature this side of hell
That gets juice from a nut,
    without cracking the shell!
                                        G. Ames

A toast:

Here's to the charmer whose dimples we prize;
    Now to the maid who has none, sir;
 Here's to the girl with a pair of blue eyes,
    And here's to the nymph with but one, sir.
        Let the toast pass -
        Drink to the lass -
I'll warrant she'll prove an excuse for the glass.

A toast:

Wine and Women -
may we always have a taste for both.

A toast:

A full purse, a fresh bottle, and a beautiful face.

A toast:

Here's a turkey when you are hungry,
    Champagne when you are dry,
A pretty girl when you need her,
    And heaven when you die!

A toast:

Here's to the glass we so love to sip,
It dries many a pensive tear;
'Tis not so sweet as a woman's lip,
But a damn sight more sincere.

A toast:

Here's to the girl I love,
I wish that she was nigh;
If drinking beer would bring her here,
I'd drink the whole place dry.

A toast:

Drink to me only with thine eyes,
    And I will pledge with mine;
Or leave a kiss but in the cup,
    And I'll not look for wine.
                                    Ben Jonson

A toast:

Here's to St. Louis, First in Shoes, First in Booze, And Last in the American League!

(God bless the Browns)

131

A toast:
We raise a glass to those
who raised us!

A toast to Grandparents:
Let us raise our glasses
And then imbibe
To the splendid couple
Who founded this tribe!

A toast:
Here's to our absent friends
- in the hopes that they,
wherever they are, are drinking to us!

A toast:
Here's to our faraway friends.
May their spirits be with us
as soon as these spirits are in us!

A Spanish toast:
Vinos y amores, los viejos son los mejores.
Wines and friends, the old ones are the best.

A toast:
Here's to cold nights, warm friends,
and a good drink to give them!

A toast:
Here's to the four hinges of Friendship -
Swearing, Lying, Stealing and Drinking.
When you swear, swear by your country;
When you lie, lie for a pretty woman;
When you steal, steal away from bad company;
And when you drink, drink with me!

A toast:
High noon behind the tamarisks -
the sun is hot above us -
As at Home the Christmas Day is breaking wan.
They will drink our healths at dinner -
those who tell us how they love us,
And forget us till another year be gone!
Rudyard Kipling
'Christmas in India'

A Long Life

A toast:
An egg of one hour,
Bread of one day,
A goat of one month,
Wine of six months,
Flesh of a year,
Fish of ten years,
A wife of
    twenty years
A friend among
    a hundred,
Are the best of
    all numbers.
John Wodroephe

132

A toast:

To the Spirit of Christmas,
May peace on Earth and
Goodwill toward men
Never be as hard to come by
As fine whiskey. *Jack Daniel*

A toast:

I wish you a Malty Christmas
  And a Hoppy New Year,
    A pocket full of money
      And a cellar full of Beer!

A toast:

Christmas has come; let every man
Eat, drink, be merry all he can.
Our whiskey's yours - let it be mine;
No matter what lies in the bowls,
We'll make it rich with our own souls.
  William Henry Davies

A toast:

Here's to the best key for unlocking
friendship - Whis-key.

A Spanish toast:
Bebe hermanos porque
  la vida es breve!
Drink brothers because
  life is short!

A toast:

Over the lips and down to the liver,
Come on whiskey - make me quiver!
  Redd Foxx

A toast:

To champagne -
  Nectar strained to finest gold,
  Sweet as love, as virtue cold.

A toast to Irish Coffee:

Irish Mist, smoothes as the
  wit of the land,
Coffee, strong as a friendly hand,
Cream, rich as an Irish brogue.

A German toast:

Trink, trink Brüderlein, trink;
Geh nicht alleine nach Haus!
Meide den Kummer und
  meide den Schmerz,
Dann ist das Lebenein Scherz!

Drink, drink, brother dear, drink;
Do not go home alone!
Avoid sorrow and pain,
And all your life will be fun!

A Old Morton Irish Toast:

Water is the strong stuff,
It carries whales and ship.
But water is the wrong stuff,
Don't let it pass your lips.
It will wet your suits,
And rust your boots, and
Put aches in all your bones,
Dilute it well with whiskey, aye,
Or leave it well alone.
  Angie Hittner

133

A toast:

Lift 'em high and drain 'em dry
To the guy who says, 'My turn to buy!'

A toast:

Here is a riddle most abstruse;
Can you read the answer right?
Why is it that my tongue grows loose,
Only when I grow tight?

A toast:

Here's to a temperance supper,
With water in glasses tall,
And coffee and tea to end with -
And me not there at all!

A toast:

Let us acknowledge the evils of alcohol
and strive to eliminate the wine cellar -
one glass at a time.

A toast:

To drinking together, the safest form
of sex ever invented.

A toast:

There are no sorrows wine cannot allay,
There are no sins wine cannot wash away,
There are no riddles wine knows not to read,
There are no debts wine is too poor to pay!

Richard Le Gallienne

A toast:

One bottle for the four of us -
Thank God there's no more of us!

A toast:

Don't die of love; in heaven above
Or hell, they'll not endure you;
Why look glum when Doctor Rum
Is waiting for to cure you?

Oliver Herford

A toast:

Here's to politicians. The distiller's true friend.
For wherever you find four politicians together,
You're sure to find a fifth.

Jack Daniel's Tour Guides

A toast:

Here's to the light heart and the heavy hand!

A toast:

What harm in drinking
can there be?
Since punch and life
so well agree?

Thomas Blacklock

A toast:

Here's to action.
You don't learn to hold
your own in the world
by standing on guard,
but by attacking and
getting well-hammered
yourself!

George Bernard Shaw

A toast:

**May we always be
as bubbly as this
champagne!**

A toast:

Wine, wit and wisdom.
Wine enough to sharpen wit,
Wit enough to give zest to wine,
Wisdom enough to 'shut down'
    at the right time.

A toast:

Some take their gold
In minted mold,
And some in harps
    hereafter,
But give me mine
In bubbles fine
And keep the change
    in laughter.

Oliver Herford

A toast:

Here's to champagne, the drink divine,
That makes us forget our troubles;
It's made of a dollar's worth of wine,
And three dollar's worth of bubbles.

A toast:

Here's to me in my sober mood,
when I ramble, sit and think.
Here's to me in my drunken mood,
when I gambol, sin and drink.
And when this world is over
and my time has come to pass,
I hope they bury me upside down
- so the world can kiss my ass!

Sgt. Harold C. Bulk

(US Air Force)

A toast:

"To my uncle,
who taught me that you should
always stop drinking
when you can't
spell your name backwards...
here's to Uncle Bob!"

Dan Chopin

A toast:

Come, come let us drink to the Vintners Good Health.
'Tis the Cask not the Coffer, that holds the true wealth.

17th century Drinking Song

135

A toast to Armagnac:

If I had a Dog who could Piss this stuff,
And if I thought He could Piss enough,
I'd strap that Puppy to my side
And suck his Dick until he Died.

Mrs. L. Bröeckmann
A delicate, elderly gentlelady.

A toast:

I wish I were a brewer's horse:
Then when the coast was clear
I'd turn my head where the tail should be
And drink up all the beer.

Anon.

*(a parody of a Precentor's rhyme, to the tune
'Crimond', from the 19th century, when it
was still considered irreverent to sing the
words of the Psalms during choir practice.)*

CHAPTER TWELVE

Drinking Stories

NATIONALITIES

The Americans are a funny lot: they drink whiskey to keep them warm; then they put some ice in it to make it cool; then they put some sugar in it to make it sweet, and then they put a slice of lemon in it to make it sour. Then they say *'here's to you'* and drink it themselves.

B. N. Chakravarty

I judge that the American is more interested in getting drunk than in drinking.

Giuseppe Giacosa

You Americans have the loveliest wines in the world, you know, but you don't realize it. You call them *domestic* and that's enough to start trouble anywhere.

H. G. Wells

I might express it somewhat abruptly by saying that most Americans are born drunk, and really require a little wine or beer to sober them. They have a sort of permanent intoxication from within, a sort of invisible champagne ... Americans do not need to drink to inspire them to do anything, though they do sometimes, I think, need a little for the deeper and more delicate purpose of teaching them how to do nothing.

G. K. Chesterton

There are two types of people that shouldn't drink, **the Irish and the Indians -** and in that order!

Ed Kelly

If not using it, they talk about it. It enters into their very characters; the father's penuriousness is most neatly summed up by the fact that he keeps his liquor under lock and key and has an **eagle eye** for the exact level of the whiskey in the bottle ... By the same token, the measure of the son's rebellion is how much liquor he can 'sneak'.

John Henry Raleigh
(on Eugene O'Neill's New England Irish-Catholic background)

It is a deadly insult to refuse to take a drink from a man, unless an elaborate explanation and apology be given and accepted.   *M. J. F. McCarthy*

They [the British] are like their own beer: froth on top, dregs at bottom, the middle excellent.

Voltaire

138

I am as **drunk as a lord**, but then, I am one, so what does it matter?

Bertrand Russell

The story goes that not long after James I acceded to the throne, a certain English nobleman gave a dinner party to which he invited a large number of luminaries. After the goblets had been filled and refilled several times and the liquor had taken hold, an English general named Somerset rose from his chair and proclaimed: "Gentlemen, when I am in my cups, and the generous wine begins to warm my blood, I have an absurd custom of railing against the Scottish people. Knowing my weakness, I hope no gentlemen in the company will take it amiss."

Having thus delivered himself, he sat down, and a Highland chief, one Sir Robert Blackie of Blair-Antholl, rose and with singular dispassion addressed his fellow celebrants as follows: "Gentlemen, when I am in my cups, and the generous wine begins to warm my blood, if I hear a man rail against the Scottish people, I have an absurd custom of kicking him at once out of the company, often breaking a few of his bones in the process. Knowing my weakness, I hope no gentlemen will take it amiss."

The story concludes, we need scarcely add, that General Somerset did not that night follow his usual custom of denigrating the Scottish people.

'Drunken Comportment'

A true German can't stand the French, Yet willingly he drinks their wines.

Johann Wolfgang von Goethe

In Spain, that land of monks and apes,
  The thing called wine
    doth come from grapes;
But on the noble river Rhine
  The thing called gripes
    doth come from wine.

Samuel Taylor Coleridge

France: the largest country in Europe, a great boon for drunks who need room to fall.

Alan Coren

I'm so holy that when I drink wine, it turns into water.

Aga Khan III

If you find an Australian indoors, it's a fair bet that he will have a glass in his hand.

Jonathan Aitken

139

The Persians are very fond of wine ... It is also their general practice to deliberate upon affairs of weight when they are drunk; and then in the morning, when they are sober, the decision to which they came the night before is put before them by the master of the house in which it was made; and if approved they act on it, if not, they set it aside. Sometimes, however, they are sober at their first deliberations, but in this case they always reconsider the matter under the influence of wine.

Herodotus

If we heard it said of Orientals that they habitually drank a liquor which went to their heads, deprived them of reason and made them vomit, we should say: "How very barbarous!"

Jean de La Bruyère

Politicians & Lawyers

An old time bellhop at Washington's Mayflower Hotel was asked if he was able to tell if a guest was a Republican or a Democrat.

"Oh, sure" he responded, "It's easy. It's in the way they fix their drinks. There's nothing to it. The Republicans measure out their drinks and the Democrats just pour."

Vincent Sardi & George She

"Your fine is ten dollars and two bits."
"Yes, Your Honor, but what's the two bits for?"
"To buy your Honorable Judge a drink this fine morning."

early California saloon court proceedings

My final warning to you is always pay for your own drinks ... All the scandals in the world of politics today have their cause in the despicable habit of swallowing free drinks.

Y. Yakigawa
President, Kyoto University
(advice to students)

"Who is the best lawyer in town?"
"Henry Brown when he is sober."
"And who is the second-best lawyer in town?"
"Henry Brown when he is drunk."

"I had not intended to discuss this controversial subject at this particular time. However, I want you to know that I do not shun controversy.

On the contrary, I will take a stand on any issue at any time, regardless of how fraught with controversy it might be.

You have asked me how I feel about whiskey.

All right, here is how I feel about whiskey ...

If, when you say whiskey, you mean the devil's brew, the poison scourge, the bloody monster that defiles innocence, dethrones reason, destroys the home, creates misery and poverty, yea, literally takes the bread from the mouths of little children;

If you mean that evil drink that topples the Christian man and woman from the pinnacle of righteous, gracious living into the bottomless pit of degradation and despair, and shame, and and helplessness, and hopelessness,

Then certainly I am against it,

But;

If, when you say whiskey, you mean the oil of conversation, the philosophic wine, the ale that is consumed when good fellows get together, that puts a song in their hearts and laughter on their lips, and the warm glow of contentment in their eyes;

If you mean the stimulating drink that puts the spring into the old gentleman's step on a frosty, crispy morning;

If you mean the drink which enables a man to magnify his joy, and his happiness, and to forget, if only for a little while, life's great tragedies, heartaches, and sorrows;

If you mean that drink, the sale of which pours into our treasuries untold millions of dollars, which are used to provide tender care for our little crippled children, our blind, our deaf, our pitiful aged and infirm; to build highways and hospitals and schools,

Then certainly, I am for it.

This is my stand, I will not retract from it, I will not compromise."

Anon.

According to former Representative D.R. Billy Mathews, this story was told in the early 1960s by another member of Congress, who did not know the author.

141

MINISTERS & THE CLERGY

Better sleep with a sober cannibal than a drunken Christian.

Herman Melville

I could have done with some strong whiskey but … all I got was dry sherry. It was but the first of many such drinks, as I found that Anglican clergy favor it above all others.

Basil Spence

The catering department mistakenly served the "Spiked Watermelon" dessert to a group of Baptist ministers. "Well," demanded the chef. "What did they say? Did they like it?"

"I don't know how they liked it," replied the waiter, "but they were dividing up the seeds and putting them in their pockets."

Some Drinking Stories & Observations

It's my opinion, sir, that this meeting is drunk.

Charles Dickens

I am sparkling; *you* are unusually talkative; *he* is drunk! *New Statesman*

You must be careful about giving any drink whatsoever to a bore. A lit-up bore is the worst in the world.

David Cecil

Sir Robert Walpole's father encouraged him to drink very deeply. For every time he filled his own glass he filled his son's glass twice. "Come, Robert," said the senior Walpole, "you shall drink twice while I drink once, for I cannot permit my son in his sober senses to witness the intoxication of his father."

Never refuse wine. It is an odd but universally held opinion that anyone who doesn't drink must be an alcoholic.

P. J. O'Rourke

Booze, of course, and then, curtains.

Kingsley Amis
(on being asked how he would spend the Booker Prize)

He neither drank, smoked, nor rode a bicycle. Living frugally, saving his money, he died early, surrounded by greedy relatives. It was a great lesson to me.

John Barrymore

The best audience is intelligent, well-educated, and a little drunk.

Alben W. Barkley

143

My dad was the town drunk.
Usually that's not so bad,
but New York City?

Henny Youngman

I came from a bunch
of Irish drunks,
my mother and father.
They had half a bag on
most of the time.

Marlon Brando

I drink too much.
Last time I gave a
urine sample
there was
an olive in it.

Rodney Dangerfield

Actually, it only takes one drink
to get me loaded.
The trouble
is I can't remember if it's
the thirteenth or fourteenth.

George Burns

Some Drunk Jokes

CHAPTER THIRTEEN

The Morning After The Night Before

WHO DRINKS TOO MUCH

An alcoholic had been lightly defined as a man who drinks more than his own doctor.
Alvan L. Barach

A productive drunk is the bane of moralists. *Anon.*

If four or five guys tell you you're drunk, even though you know you haven't had a thing to drink, the least you can do is to lie down a little while.
Joseph Schenk

An alcoholic is someone you don't like who drinks as much as you do. *Dylan Thomas*

Drunks are rarely amusing unless they know some good songs and lose a lot at poker.
Karyl Roosevelt

There is no such thing as an alcoholic, he's just a better customer. - **It's just a matter of perspective.**
Tom Burnham
(Saloonkeeper)

Grant stood by me when I was crazy, and I stood by him when he was drunk, and now we stand by each other.
William Tecumseh Sherman

There is a distinct lack of concern on the part of management. It's paranoia on their part. They want to keep it quiet and out of the newspapers. They want you to believe that nothing like this could ever happen in their organization.
Don Newcombe
(on organized baseball's attitude toward alcoholism)

A buffoon is a drunk on a hitting spree. A drunk is a pitcher who's lost his fast ball. A confirmed drunk is a pitcher with a sore arm. An incurable drunk is a pitcher who hasn't won a game all season.
Leo Durocher

When I played drunks I had to remain sober because I didn't know how to play them when I was drunk.
Richard Burton

If you are young and you drink a great deal it will spoil your health, slow your mind, make you fat - in other words, turn you into an adult. Also, if you want to get one of those great red beefy, impressive-looking faces that politicians and corporation presidents have, you had better start drinking early and stick with it.
P. J. O'Rourke

There are three things that are not to be credited: a woman when she weeps, a merchant when he swears, nor a drunkard when he prays.

Barnabe Rich

If merely 'feeling good' could decide, drunkenness would be the supremely valid human experience.

William James

A drunkard is like a whiskey bottle, all neck and belly and no head.

Austin O'Malley

I ask them [Navajo youth], "what is your biggest problem?" They tell me alcohol, drugs. I ask them, "What is the most beautiful machine? They tell me they don't know how to answer.

I tell them it's their heads, and they must not let alcohol and drugs ruin that machine."

Annie Dodge Wauneka

Drunkenness is never anything but a substitute for happiness. It amounts to buying the dream of a thing when you haven't money enough to buy the dreamed-of thing materially.

André Gide

The second group are the real dipsomaniacs, those who cannot resist drinking because of a craving. Behind this craving will always be found, I think, some deep-rooted mental or physical cause. Sometimes this state is produced or aggravated by a severe mental depression, an unhappy love affair often, or the loss of money. It may be a temporary condition that passes after a few months or less, or it may be permanent. Drinking is a relief from the responsibilities of life, an outlet from reality, an escape that may be vitally necessary in order to avoid suicide.

Jimmie Charters

MAN, ANIMALS & DRINK

The first glass makes a man animated, his vivacity great, his colors heightened. In this condition he is like a peacock. When the fumes of the liquor rise into his head, he is gay, leaps and gambols as an ape. Drunkenness takes possession of him, he is like a furious lion. When it is at its height he is like the swine; he falls and grovels on the ground, stretches himself out and goes to sleep.

ancient Mohammedan tradition

147

When man eats the fruit of the vine he is as gentle as a lamb; when he drinks wine he believes himself a lion; if, by chance, he drinks too much he grimaces like a monkey; and when he is often drunk he is nothing more than a **vile pig**.
The Talmud

When Women Drink Too Much

It's bad enough to see a man drunk - but a woman!
American proverb

A drunken woman **IS AN OPEN DOOR.**
German proverb

In our society, we get to know one another over drinks, we associate feasts and celebrations with liquor. We think we have to drink, that it's a social necessity ... It's romantic as long as you can handle it - for years I could and did - but it's misery when you become addicted.
Betty Ford

One drink, and I'm yours;
Two drinks and I'm anybody's;
Three drinks, and then
Away goes Mother's good advice.
Anon.

"My country, right or wrong" is a thing that no patriot would think of saying, except in a desperate case. It is like saying "My mother, drunk or sober."
G. K. Chesterton

"DRINKING TOO MUCH AIN'T BAD"

It's all right letting yourself go as long as you can let yourself back.
Mick Jagger

I never drink while I'm working, but after a few glasses, I get ideas that would never have occurred to me dead sober. And some of the ideas turn out to be valuable the next day. Some not.
Irwin Shaw

DRINKING & THE GODS

Drunkenness is a joy reserved for the gods; so men do partake of it impiously, and so they are very properly punished for their audacity.
James Branch Cabell

DRINKING AND THE DEVIL

There is in all men a demand for superlative, so much so that the poor devil who has no other way of reaching it attains it by getting drunk.

Oliver Wendall Holmes

Where Satan cannot go in person, there he sends wine.

Jewish proverb

Strong drink is not only the devil's way into a man, but man's way to the devil.

Adam Clarke

No power on earth or above the bottomless pit has such influence to terrorize and make cowards of men as the liquor power. Satan could not have fallen on a more potent instrument with which to thrall the world. Alcohol is king!

Eliza "Mother" Stewart
(1816 - 1908) US temperance leader

DRUNKENNESS & DEATH

Drunkenness is the ruin of reason. It is premature old age. It is temporary death.

St. Basil

Drunkenness is temporary suicide: the happiness that it brings is merely negative, a momentary cessation of unhappiness.

Bertrand Russell

DRINKING & DRIVING

If you Drink, don't Drive. Don't even Putt! *Dean Martin*

Death by drunken driving is a socially acceptable form of homicide.

Candy Lightner

Victims of drunk drivers have no place to turn. Judges drink and drive, juries drink and drive, D.A.'s drink and drive. They're going to have sympathy for the drunk driver. They don't have sympathy for the rapist, the murderer, the mugger.

Candy Lightner

149

There are two groups of people in the world now. Those that get pathetically drunk in public - and the rest of us poor bastards who are expected to drive these **pinheads** home.

Dennis Miller

You shouldn't drink and drive. If you get drunk, don't call a cab. That costs you twenty dollars or forty dollars or fifty dollars. Do what I do. Call a tow truck. It might cost a little more, but your car will be there when you wake up.

Jeffrey Jena

Are we taking the drunken drivers off the road only to turn them into drunken pedestrians?

Lawrence S. Harris

Arresting a single drunk or a single vagrant who has harmed no identifiable person seems so unjust, and in a sense it is. But failing to do anything about a score of drunks or a hundred vagrants may destroy an entire community.

James Q. Wilson

WHEN IN DOUBT, DON'T START OUT.

(New York State Drivers Association Warning motorists not to drink and drive)

Gasoline and alcohol don't mix - but try drinking them straight.

Anon.

By all means, let's breath-test pedestrians involved in road accidents - if they're still breathing.

The Bishop of Ely

In the latter days of the saloon it was the custom for the house to buy the fourth drink. After the automobile became popular this habit was dropped, honest publicans being averse to becoming accessories to drunken driving and its appalling results. Some saloonkeepers feeling an explanation might be expected displayed signs reading: "You give us your car keys and we'll give you the fourth drink."

Jim Marshall

Take three chorus girls and three men, soak in champagne till midnight, squeeze into an automobile. Add a dash of joy, and a drunken chauffeur,. Shake well. Serve at 70 miles an hour. Chaser: a coroner's inquest.

a 1920s recipe

Don't drink and drive. You may hit a bump and spill your drink.

Anon.

DRINKING, FIGHTING & CRIME

He that kills a man when he is drunk shall be hanged when he is sober.
proverb

It's not that Billy drinks a lot. It's just that he fights a lot when he drinks a little. *Dick Young*
(on Billy Martin)

... if you are abusive of yourself and others when you drink, then alcohol is not for you. You should quit before you harm yourself or someone else. If you find yourself drinking only for effect, you should seek counseling.

Fred Eckhardt

I think those who can drink them [spirits] and do not, fools, but I think those who can't drink them and do, worse fools and unjust men too because they bring scandal on an excellent creature and consume that share of it that should go to others. *George Saintsbury*

The variety of drunken behavior is the same as that of madmen; some of them being raging, others loving, other laughing, all extravagantly, but according to their several domineering passions.
Thomas Hobbes

'Tis not the drinking that is blamed, but the excess. *John Selden*

Get the best of liquor or it will get the best of you.
Anon.

WHAT HAPPENS TO DRUNKS

Drunkenness makes some men fools, some beasts, and some devils.
H. C. Bohn

If we take habitual drunkards as a class, their heads and their hearts will bear an advantageous comparison with those of any other class. There seems ever to have been a proneness in the brilliant and warm-blooded to fall into this life. The demon of intemperance ever seems to have delighted in sucking the blood of genius and generosity.
Abraham Lincoln

Alcoholism isn't a spectator sport. Eventually the whole family gets to play. *Joyce R. Burditt*

151

He smiled a kind of sickly smile,
and curled up on the floor,
And the subsequent proceedings
interested him no more.
Francis Brett Harte

There are two kinds of people I can't stand: A sober person when I'm drunk or a drunk person when I'm sober.
David A. Hudson

The worst thing about some men is that when they are not drunk they are sober.
William Butler Yeats

A drinking man is the last to be hired and the first to be fired.
Anon.

The sight of a drunkard is a better sermon against that vice than the best that was ever preached on that subject.
Saville

Alcoholics lie.

It is intrinsic. They lie to their friends, they lie to themselves, they even lie to other alcoholics. Non-addicted drinkers often brag about how much they drink; alcoholics almost always minimize it. This is not to say that the alcoholic is basically dishonest. He may be a model of virtue in all things, except where his drinking is concerned. But this is misleading, because almost every decision an alcoholic makes is influenced by its possible effect on his ability to get a drink, now or two weeks hence.
Art Hill

Drunkenness is an **immoderate affection** and use of drink. That I call immoderation that is besides or beyond that order of good things for which God hath given us the use of drink.
Jeremy Taylor

One evening in October,
When I was far from sober,
And dragging home a load
with manly pride,
My feet began to stutter
So I laid down in the gutter
And a pig came up and
parked right by my side.
Then I warbled, "It's fair weather
When good fellows get together,"
Till a lady passing by was
heard to say:
"You can tell a man who boozes
By the company he chooses!"
Then the pig got up and
slowly walked away.
*Benjamin H. Burt and
Aimor A. Dickson*

The best cure for drunkenness is while sober to see a drunken man.
Chinese proverb

152

Few things surpass old wine; and they preach
Who pleases, - the more because they preach in vain, -
Let us have wine and women, mirth and laughter,
Sermons and soda-water the day after.

Lord Byron

If the hangover came the night before and the elation the morning after, **brewers would be out of business.** The principle that a lesser but early benefit will offset a substantial but postponed liability is one which rules human life; indeed it is the principle on which the human race reproduces itself.

The Times

I never played drunk,
hungover, yes,
but never drunk.

Hack Wilson
(Chicago Cubs outfielder)

Dense sleep doesn't fade a wine hangover.

Li Ch'ing-chao

A mouth like the inside of a zookeepers welly.

Peter Watson

I remember, I remember
   Nothing further after that,
But I wakened in the morning
   On an alien lobby mat,
And I felt not unpersuaded
   (Though my reasons were not clear)
That I'd spent a merry Christmas
   And a prosperous New Year.

George Fletcher

He resolved, having done it once, never to move his eyeballs again.

Kingsley Amis

Best Hangover Cure:
Go to bed for three days with a good book or somebody who's read one.

Mark Pollman

153

A dusty thudding in his head made the scene before him beat like a pulse. His mouth had been used as a latrine by some small creature of the night and then as its mausoleum.

Kingsley Amis

The hangover is something to occupy the head that wasn't used the night before. *Anon.*

Drunken days have all their tomorrows.

Samuel Smiles

CHAPTER FOURTEEN

Temperance & Prohibition

Drinking Lightly & Abstaining

Dinner parties were problems because I was always explaining myself.
No, I don't drink, thank you.
Not even *wine*?
Nothing, thanks.
But *why*?
I have no talent for it, I said.

Pete Hamill

The secret to a long life is to stay busy, get plenty of exercise, and don't drink too much. Then again, don't drink too little!

Hermann Smith-Johannson

Like a camel, I can go without a drink for seven days - and have on several horrible occasions

Herb Caen

He's the only poet that I've ever known in the universe who simply did not drink.

John Berryman
(on Randall Jarrell)

It's alright to drink like a Fish; As long as you drink what a Fish drinks.

Jim Morrison

Islam prohibits alcoholic drinks ... drinking makes people lose their heads and impedes clear thinking. Even music dulls the mind.

Ayatollah Khomeini

Take that liquor away; I never touch strong drink. I like it too well to fool with it.

Stonewall Jackson
(responding to an offer of a mint julep, 1864)

There are, I believe, some of you who never touch alcohol in any shape or form. I respect your convictions wholeheartedly, but I am sincerely sorry for you at the same time. For when you wake up in the morning that's as good as you're ever gonna feel.

Robert Mitchum

156

Temperance And Moderation

Drink not the third glass,
  which thou canst not tame,
When once it is within thee.
George Herbert

A man who seldom takes more than one drink explained: "One drink is just right, two are too many and three are not enough." *Anon.*

If wine were made accessible to all classes in this country, temperance societies would soon be superfluous. For when the frugal meal of our humble labourer and artisan is cheered (as elsewhere) by a wholesome and invigorating beverage, drunkenness will gradually disappear.

"Wine in Relation to Temperance"

The first glass for myself;
the second for my friends;
the third for good humor;
and the fourth for mine enemies.
Sir William Temple

Boys should abstain from all use of wine until their eighteenth year, for it is wrong to add fire to fire. *Plato*

Abstinence & Swearing Off

Teetotalers lack the sympathy and generosity of men that drink.
W. H. Davies

When you teetotal, you've got an awful feeling that everybody's your boss.
Will Fyffe

A lady temperance candidate concluded her passionate oration, "I would rather commit adultery than take a glass of beer." Whereupon a clear voice from the audience asked "Who wouldn't?"
Adlai E. Stevenson

It ought to give pause to the most fanatical teetotaler that the only humans worth saving in the Flood were **a family of vintners**.
Dr Bernard Rudofsky

If a man deliberately abstains from wine to such an extant that he does serious harm to his nature, he will not be free from blame.

Saint Thomas Aquinas

157

The man who chooses to be a total abstainer is to be respected. In some cases it is a wise precaution, even an imperative duty, to abstain; but the man who would thrust total abstinence on everybody else is misguided. He errs in equating total abstinence with temperance and in refusing to learn the lesson of experience - that prohibition tends to encourage the very evils it seeks to destroy.

F. Marian McNeill

The **dipsomaniac** and the abstainer are not only both mistaken, but they both make the same mistake. They both regard wine as a drug, and not a drink.

G. K. Chesterton

Drink and the world drinks with you; swear off and you drink alone.

Anon.

Have you ever heard of a teetotaler conspicuous for kindliness of heart, or intellectually distinguished in any walk of life? I should be glad to know his name. A sorry crew! Not because they drink water, but because the state of mind which makes them dread alcohol is unpropitious to the hatching of any generous idea.

Norman Douglas

I once shook hands with Pat Boone and my whole right side *sobered up.*

Dean Martin

Sobriety's a real turn-on for me. You can see what you're doing.

Peter O'Toole

An old stomach reforms more whiskey drinkers than a new resolve.

Don Marquis

On New Year's Day, some years ago,
I swore off alcohol;
And, one year later, I eschewed
Pipes, cigarettes, et al.
The next, I quit profanity
As something not too nice.
And then abandoned slot machines,
Card games, roulette and dice.
Thus curing faults each year, I reached
A state of such perfection
That I have not a single flaw
Now calling for correction.
But New Year's Day is now for me
A ruined Institution;
For what is New Year's Day without
A New Year's resolution?

Leverett Lyon

AA is no success story in the ordinary sense of the word. It is a story of suffering transmuted, under grace, into spiritual progress.

Bill Wilson
(cofounder, Alcoholics Anonymous)

Many men give up drinking on account of the wife and bad kidneys.

Anon.

There should be asylums for habitual teetotalers, but they would probably relapse into teetotalism as soon as they came out.

Samuel Butler

There is much less drinking now than there was before 1927, because I quit drinking on May 24, 1927.

Rabbit Maranville

PROHIBITION & PROHIBITIONISTS

Spirits are what men will not do without. To prohibit them and secure total abstinence from them is beyond the power even of sages.

Ancient Chinese record

Prohibition will work great injury to the cause of temperance. It is a species of intemperance within itself, for it goes beyond the bounds of reason in that it attempts to control a man's appetite by legislation, and makes a crime out of things that are not crimes. A Prohibition law strikes a blow at the very principles upon which our government was founded.

John B. Goodwin
(wrongly attributed to Abraham Lincoln)

A one-legged prohibition agent on a bicycle could stop the beer in the Loop in a day - if he were honest.

Peetie Wheatstraw

I see where they now propose to stop cigarettes first and then profanity. They are going to have a rough time with that profanity, cause along as there is a prohibitionist living there will be profanity.

Will Rogers

Personally I think the saloon men put this prohibition through, as they have sold more in the last year than in any ten previous years before.

Will Rogers

Prohibition has made nothing but trouble.

Al Capone

159

PROHIBITIONS

1. 1736 to 1742, the Gin Act was put into enforcement in England.
2. 1735 to 1742, the state of Georgia prohibited 'hard liquor'.
3. 1908 to 1934, Iceland prohibited drinking (the longest of 26 years).
4. 1914 to 1924, Russia prohibited drinking.
5. January 16, 1920 to Tuesday 6:55 pm, December 5, 1933, *The Volstead Act* was in effect in the United States for 13 years, 10 months, 17 hours and 32 and 1/2 minutes.

There is a crying for wine in the streets; all joy is darkened, the mirth of the land is gone.
Isaiah XXIV

ALL NATIONS WELCOME EXCEPT CARRY

old saloon sign

... many teetotalers are now moderate tipplers in that the sipping of an illegal cocktail is spiced with adventure. ... They are told they mustn't do this or that, so they just lay back their ears and go ahead and do all the things forbidden, just to prove that they are unshackled freemen and no one can tell them where to get off.

George Ade

The prohibition law, written for weaklings and derelicts, has divided the nation, like Gaul, into three parts - wets, drys and hypocrites. *Pauline Morton Sabu*

When by mere legislation, man can stop fruit from fermenting of its own accord after it falls to the ground he can talk about a law of prohibition. The very word destroys its meaning. You can't prohibit nature. *E. Temple Thurston*

The country couldn't run with prohibition. That is the industrial fact.

Henry Ford

160

Because Milwaukee was a German town the saloon was never an evil institution. Even preachers were horrified when Carry Nation arrived. John Callahan kept a saloon on Grand Avenue near West Water Street. He was always spoken of as *'Honest John'* and was one of the few who deserved that common title. Until he got too old he refereed prize fights. No one ever made a bet without having John for stakeholder and all matters of a sporting nature went to him for final irrevocable decision. The city was proud of John and his reputation. When Carry appeared with her axe, John did not ask the police for protection. The lady never got inside the door. She got it square between the eyes, and in both of them, and she kept on getting it until she ran. John could see no reason why an honest, respectable establishment should be wrecked by *'a crazy nut from Kansas'* - and he made sure it wasn't.

Jim Marshall

I'm wetter than the middle of the Atlantic Ocean.

Big Bill Thompson
(Chicago's Prohibition Era Mayor)

Al Capone

I'm out of the booze racket now and I wish the papers would let me alone. I'm a businessman. I made my money by supplying a popular demand. If I break the law my customers are as guilty as I am. When I sell liquor it's bootlegging. When my patrons serve it on silver trays on Lake Shore Drive it's hospitality. The country wanted booze and I've organized it. Why should I be called a public enemy? *Al Capone*

All I ever did was to sell beer and whiskey to our best people. All I ever did was to supply a demand that was pretty popular.
Al Capone

I am going to St. Petersburg, Florida, tomorrow. Let the worthy citizens of Chicago get their liquor the best they can. I'm off the job - it's a thankless one and full of grief. I've been spending the best years of my life as a public benefactor. *Al Capone*

161

Prohibition only
drives drunkenness
behind doors
and into dark
places, and does
not cure it or
even diminish it.

Mark Twain

Although man is already **ninety per cent** water,
the Prohibitionists are not yet satisfied.

John Kendrick Bangs

A prohibitionist is the sort of man one
wouldn't care to drink with, even if he drank.

H. L. Mencken

There aint gonna be no whiskey; there aint gonna be no gin;
There aint gonna be no highball to put the highball in;
There aint gonna be no cigarettes to make folks pale and thin;
But you can't take away that tendency to sin, sin, sin.

Vaughn Miller

162

Prohibition makes you want to cry into your beer and denies you the beer to cry into.

Don Marquis

in the British tradition:

"Time, Gentlemen, please!"

———— ◆ ————

"Boys & Girls, you know that I love you - but guess what time it is?"

———— ◆ ————

"Thanks Folks, But That's All There Is - For Now!"

Mark Pollman

163

For correspondence,
adding quotes or
comments,
contact Mark Pollman at
Wildstone Media
POBox 511580
St Louis, MO 63151

INDEX

166

170